CORDON Vʋ

Elegant dinner parties for the vegetarian
host-in-a-hurry.

By the same author
THORSONS VEGETARIAN MICROWAVE COOKBOOK

CORDON

Vitesse

**Elegant Dinner Parties for the Vegetarian
Host-in-a-Hurry**

CECILIA NORMAN

THORSONS PUBLISHING GROUP

First published in 1988

Colour photography and styling by
Paul Turner and Sue Pressley,
Stonecastle Graphics, Maidstone.
Text illustrations by Paul Turner.

British Library Cataloguing in Publication Data

Norman, Cecilia
  Cordon Vitesse.
  1. Vegetarian cookery   2. Dinners and
  dining
  I. Title
  641.5'636   TX837

  ISBN 0-7225-1515-4

*Published by Thorsons Publishers Limited,
Wellingborough, Northamptonshire, NN8 2RQ, England*

Printed in Great Britain by
Hazell, Watson and Viney Limited,
Member of BPCC plc, Aylesbury, Buckinghamshire

10 9 8 7 6 5 4 3 2 1

Contents

Acknowledgements

I would like to thank Penny Morris for her help with recipe testing and menu planning, which is a much harder task than one would imagine; Colin Lambert, an expert on the art of Indian cookery, for the curry recipes, my husband Laurie for the many hours spent dictating recipes and putting the chapters in order, and Jenny Pouncett who laboured at the typewriter behind the scenes and at the same time picked up any errors that might otherwise have slipped through our checking system.

1 Planning to be Quick

There are two kinds of cookbook: the fantasy one which is for browsing and the other from which you cook. This book is for the busy person who likes to entertain. Now busy people — and aren't we all — do have occasional days when we can cook in quantity and put away in the freezer for either planned or emergency needs. This kind of preparation cannot include dishes ready for immediate serving and they will need to be titivated before taking to the table. The dishes may be perfectly acceptable for just you and yours but will almost certainly not be pretty enough for dinner parties.

To be both entertaining and speedy you need to be something of a magician. Use your freezer as your magic box and with sleight of hand make your dinner parties or supper parties seem brilliant and effortless. The freezer is not the only storage place. You can buy some 'treasures' in cans, and dry goods, such as pasta, come in pretty colours and shapes and keep exceedingly well.

The vegetarian relies also on grains, e.g. buckwheat, couscous, millet and brown rice, and these are very good keepers. Dry beans have a limited shelf life and the older they become the longer they take to cook. Nevertheless, after cooking they will keep either in the refrigerator for a few days or in the freezer almost as long as you wish. Also you can keep them ticking over for a few days if you rinse them in cold water twice a day, for instance night and morning, so that you remember when to do it. Sprouted beans need the same regular treatment and take a few days to sprout. (See pages 22–3 in Chapter 3.) They are not only good for you but are remarkably attractive for garnishing.

There is nothing quite like fresh foods and I am banking on you being able to obtain these in the lunch hour or on your way home from work. It is very difficult to prepare a recipe book for everybody — if you live in a major city you are going to be able to obtain just about every ingredient. How lucky are those that dwell in the vicinity of Nine Elms, the home of the fruit and vegetable market. If you are rich enough and Harrods is your local shop then you can get just about everything, so all those exotic fruits and vegetables flown in morning fresh can be on your dinner table that evening.

I was a total town dweller until last year when I found myself spending more and more time in the country. It was hard to believe that all those people were growing all sorts of unusual vegetables in their gardens. Morning fresh takes on another meaning for me now.

There is usually a health food shop somewhere not too far from your home or work, even if you can only make time to go occasionally. Some of these shops sell all sorts of ready-to-eat foods: vegetable patties, onion bhajis and the like. Do not disdain buying these ready-cooked if you have no time to prepare them yourself. A patty topped with a grilled tomato half, served with a border of tricolour rice which you have just cooked, can be most acceptable. To do this, divide the rice between three bowls and tint with different vegetable colourings.

I have devoted the first part of the book to ideas and suggestions for basic preparations which can be stored. I have included a short list of herbs and spices which I find indispensable in my store cupboard. If you can grow your own herbs, flavours will always be better and colours brighter. You must treat them well if you are growing them in the house or they will die. Place them on a sunny window-sill but not directly in the sunlight. Feed them regularly and don't forget to water them during the growing season. A fairly humid atmosphere is best, which you can get by standing the pots in trays or bowls of moist gravel and then spraying regularly with water. Give plenty of fresh air during warm weather but don't leave them in a draught.

Food inevitably looks better on beautiful crockery, and good cutlery gives a touch of class. Look-alikes, made in such places as Japan or Taiwan, are inexpensive and somewhat better looking than the 'garage' giveaways.

The main part of the book is, as you might expect, the recipe section. These have been separated into no cook recipes (**NC**), those that take less than three-quarters of an hour to cook (**QC**) and recipes prepared ahead (**PA**). If you are going to present a three-course meal you will certainly be under pressure to get the lot done in three-quarters of an hour, so you will have to mix the menus, using some from each section.

Starters can sometimes double up as main courses or be served alongside the main dish for variety. Plain cooked vegetables should be served additionally where relevant. This mix and match type of dinner will give the greatest flexibility and the menu suggestions with all the various permutations are at the end of the book.

Also, I should say that non-vegetarians can use the recipes equally well, adding dishes of their own choice. The vegetarian diet is most varied, consisting of vegetables, nuts, fruit, rice and grains and pulses with vegetable fats and oils. Additionally eggs and cheese, milk and milk products, such as butter and cheese, made with non-animal rennet and eggs are part of the vegetarian, although not the vegan, diet. A mixture of all these foods will provide a well-balanced diet. When you are preparing dishes for a dinner or supper party or just something extra special for yourself, you need to be less concerned with the nutritional aspect. After all, you can eat better balanced foods the rest of the week. The recipes in this book range from the plain to the rich and I unashamedly include cream wherever I think it will improve the dish. Although you may not care to use cream in your normal everyday diet, you are surely entitled to a little luxury when dining with friends. There are some recipes which will not work as well using brown sugar and for these I use white sugar. Flour is usually wholemeal, but there again I do make pastry with half wholemeal and half white flour because it is much less heavy.

Those of us who are short on time have to be long in imagination. You don't necessarily have to hunt around for exotic ingredients to impress. The most important factor in producing delicious and eye-catching food is care. Attention to detail as far as garnishing and decorating are concerned can make or mar a dish, and a £10 tin of truffles sniffed out of the ground in Périgord would not look anything at all if just thrown on to the food. However, a cheap button mushroom from the local grocer, beautifully sculpted, may not add flavour but will certainly add panache.

Note: In this book butter and margarine are interchangeable and milk may be whole or skimmed, cow's or plant. Pepper is freshly milled and sea salt is recommended. Eggs are large. All spoons are level.

2 The Store Cupboard and Equipment

Apart from spices, herbs, beans, grains and nuts, the following are useful ingredients to have at hand:

vegetable stock cubes
sunflower oil (keep cool)
walnut or sesame seed oil (keep cool)
butter (refrigerated or frozen)
soft margarine (refrigerated or frozen)
dried and canned milk (whether cow's or plant)

peppercorns
sea salt
garlic salt
paprika
cayenne
curry powder
baking powder
cornflour
French mustard
English mustard

tomato purée
Holbrook's sauce
Tabasco (does not keep too well)
soya or shoyu sauce
commercial mayonnaise (store in the door of the refrigerator)

A well-stocked store cupboard and freezer are indispensable to all who cannot shop daily — but if badly stocked they are a waste of money and a waste of space.

There are plenty of basic items which keep almost for ever, but there will be some deterioration over a long period. Impulse buying is rarely a good idea and until recently, when I embarked on this book, the cupboard in my kitchen (I am not fortunate enough to have an old-fashioned walk-in larder) had more than one shelf taken up with unusual but fairly useless bits and pieces. Many of these I had bought while on holiday abroad, thinking they would help me produce stunning dishes. In practice I was unable to translate completely successfully from the various foreign languages — Faroese was particularly difficult! So when it comes to it I am hesitant to use these ingredients. But I couldn't throw them away could I, as I had paid good money for them? Amongst my collection is a vegetarian jelly mix, a custard powder, a couple of packets of corn meal, potato flakes, some kind of evil-smelling oil from Iceland and two unopened cans, now without even any labels.

Here at home I invested in a huge number of dried herbs which I obviously couldn't use all at once and now have about half a dozen jars of faded herbs, all of which have developed the same smell.

I have now turned over a new leaf and don't buy any unusual item unless I can understand the instructions and have a recipe that includes it. Buy in

13

sherry
brandy
bottle of red wine
bottle of white wine (use some
and drink the rest)

molasses
syrups
jams
marmalade

wholemeal rolls and bread (in
the freezer)

agar-agar
arrowroot

small amount grated Parmesan
(store in the refrigerator)
larger quantities of grated
Cheddar cheese (must be
stored in the freezer)

cans of vegetables: tomatoes,
tomato juice, beans, sweetcorn

Home prepared store items
breadcrumbs (fresh and dried)
croûtons
vinaigrette and salad dressings
(best kept in the cool)
cooked rice (keep in the
freezer)
cooked beans (keep in the
freezer)
cooked split peas and lentils
sautéed onions (useful at any
time to save sautéeing the
onion first and should be stored
frozen in small amounts)

small quantities unless you are sure you will be repeatedly using the ingredient. I check the 'use by' date and storage instructions and in the case of dried herbs I don't purchase a jar labelled with a date in the relatively near future. I always look at the colour of herbs as they can fade even before the expiry date if they have already been exposed to bright light in the store. Spices seem to keep their flavour well but I inspect the packages carefully as mine must be waterproof underneath, for I tend to put them down on wet surfaces when cooking.

The vegetarian is heavily reliant on beans and peas and I have a collection of these. Dried beans are more often than not sold in 1 lb/455g packs and this is quite sufficient for about eight servings. When they have been on the shelf for a very long time they become even more wrinkled and dry and then take an age to cook. Health food shops have a better turnover rate than smaller grocers' shops so I tend to shop there even if sometimes they are a little more expensive.

The varieties that are most often featured in recipes are red kidney beans, butter beans, soya beans, haricot beans, cannellini beans, borlotti beans and chick peas; but there are lots of others and they all have their differences in flavour and colour. Consider adding rose-cocoa and flageolet beans to your collection. The former are a pretty pink speckled colour and the flageolet are a delicate green.

Lentils, whether whole or split, and split peas keep very well for months and months. Because they are so versatile and easy to cook they feature widely in the non-vegetarian diet. Many varieties are also suitable for sprouting. Amongst my favourites are chick peas which taste like hazelnuts, whole mung beans used for commercial beansprouts and aduki beans which have shiny red ¼ inch/5mm barrels with single white markings. Only whole beans can be sprouted.

Of the seeds, sunflower, pumpkin and sesame are my choices and I buy huge quantities because I find them irresistible as nibbles, especially when toasted, roasted or microwaved. They can be ground or used in small proportions with flour. Sunflower and pumpkin seeds are good in casseroles and as toppings and sesame seeds (the chief ingredient in tahini paste) are available either in a pale or black colour and are usually sprinkled on dishes as a final garnish. These seeds cannot be sprouted but alfalfa are used only for sprouting as they are hard and gritty.

As far as cereals and grains are concerned, buckwheat, roast buckwheat, bulgur and millet can often be interchanged with rice and are quicker to cook. Wholewheat is nutty and can be cooked in the same way as brown rice or alternatively it can be sprouted. Both white and brown rice are regular standbys and when stored in a dry place rice can keep for several months. Brown rice and pasta can vary quite considerably in the time they take to cook, however. Long-grain brown rice is usually quicker than short-grain. Fresh pasta cooks in moments while dried pasta may take ten or fifteen minutes. With so many types available the only safe way is to follow the directions on the packet.

Nuts of all varieties and dried fruit can be stored in the refrigerator or freezer. Freezer-stored nuts, provided they are very well wrapped, will keep for ages. Wholemeal flour does not keep well in a store cupboard so to prevent rancidity keep it in the refrigerator.

Garlic salt and garlic granules store virtually for ever. Garlic salt is fine when you just want a light sprinkling and does save crushing fresh garlic, but it *is* salt and the more you use the saltier the food becomes. Garlic granules on the other hand are garlic alone without any salt.

Kitchen Equipment

The amount of equipment you have must be governed by the availability of space as much as the availability of cash. I consider the liquidizer or food processor to be probably the most important item as there is so much in the preparation of vegetarian food that can be speeded up by the use of a liquidizer or food processor. The liquidizer produces smoother soups and is excellent for mayonnaise and the processor can be used for chopping, grating, mixing and puréeing the coarser ingredients.

Hand-held electric blenders are preferred by some but detested by others. I find they blend exceedingly well but if lifted even slightly out of the mixture there is instant splattering everywhere. Great care has to be taken when washing the blade. You *must* make sure the electricity is switched off at the socket as the slightest conceivable touch on the rocker switch activates the blade. If you haven't any form of liquidizer or blender you will have to chop or beat the ingredients very finely. A useful mechanical device as a partial substitute is the mouli-légumes.

Smaller kitchen gadgets that I find useful include a hand-held lemon juicer, a tulip-shaped electric bulb on a stalk; a potato baller (not only for potatoes but also for melon, butter or any small soft garnishes); an old-fashioned upright grater comes in handy for cheese and vegetables; a zester will coarsely grate citrus peel in no time at all and is considerably easier to wash up than the multi-purpose kind; a potato masher is efficient for most mashing jobs but not for puréeing; a grapefruit knife, because of its curved end, can be used to remove flesh from melon peel, to cut the core and pulp of tomatoes, the centres from jacket potatoes etc.; tongs are helpful for dealing with delicate or hot foods and a fish slice and a slotted spoon for carefully lifting and draining; kitchen scissors for chopping; an apple corer; a couple of skewers and lastly a set of measuring spoons are all included in my equipment.

The microwave is essential to me as a career person with little time to entertain. Apart from the obvious advantages of defrosting and reheating, I use it for making sauces, scrambling eggs, stewing fruit, cooking rice, pasta and grains (but not the kidney bean family, because these require cooking for ten minutes at a full rolling boil). Also the microwave is the best for cooking vegetables. Preparation time is definitely speeded up as the microwave can be put to work on parts of a recipe while the other stages are cooked conventionally.

Quick cooking often requires more pans so that the different dishes can be cooked at the same time. The pressure cooker can sometimes be used with the separators that come with it.

A large roll of non-stick vegetable parchment heads my list of wrappings as food does not stick to it and it saves washing and scouring baking trays. Cling film and foil are needed for covering and wrapping and I always keep some square plastic boxes and thick polythene bags for freezing. Rubber bands are easier to use than the plastic ties. Labels written with a freezer pen do not smear so this is better than an ordinary biro. You are bound to have at least one roll of kitchen paper handy but make certain you have another spare in the cupboard. A large wooden chopping board and a set of sharp knives with a knife sharpener or steel are a must. Blunt knives are the likeliest cause of accidents and shiny chopping boards increase the chance of the knife slipping.

Finally, burn cream and a few plasters should be kept in the drawer, just in case!

3 Basic Preparations

Your dinner party is a last-minute decision — you turn up a suitable recipe and find that a sub-recipe has to be prepared first. This is very frustrating, particularly if it had not been included in the shopping list. It may not even be a store-cupboard preparation. Perhaps the recipe calls for 'cooked' rice or even worse 'cooked' beans which cannot by any stretch of the imagination be called quick cook.

Many basic recipes can be prepared whenever you have time to spare and they can be stored as dry goods in jars or in the freezer. Home-made additive-free mayonnaise and ready-mixed vinaigrette are superior to the commercial kinds. In this chapter there are instructions for their preparation plus some others that come in useful.

Breadcrumbs

Fresh breadcrumbs must be stored in the freezer as in the refrigerator breadcrumbs have a shorter life than bread. Pack in bags or boxes as soon as the bread is grated to prevent drying out. Breadcrumbs will keep in the freezer for about one month.

To prepare raspings or dried crumbs bake bread slices until they turn into rusks. Grate finely and store in a screw-top jar for one week or in a bag in the freezer for up to three months.

Grated Cheese

A box of home-grated cheese is a useful standby. Pack *very* loosely in a freezer box, otherwise you will find it lumpy and difficult to separate.

Egg Whites

Yolks do not freeze well but left-over egg whites frozen in small boxes keep for many months. Just be sure you label the box with the number of whites it contains. Egg whites thaw quickly and can be used for binding, as extra bulk in soufflés and for meringues.

Herbs

Herbs are freezable or can be dried at home. When thawed (except rosemary and similar spiky herbs) herbs become limp, making them suitable for use in cookery but not as garnishes. Mint and similar leafy herbs will dry out sufficiently for dry storage in a warm kitchen. Herbs can be dried in a cool oven or in the microwave provided the directions in your microwave cookbook are correctly followed.

Lemon Juice

Bottled lemon juice or the plastic lemon-shaped kind contain preservatives and are suitable only when a squeeze is required. Juice fresh lemons when at their cheapest and freeze the juice in ice cube trays. When frozen store in freezer bags. Each cube is the equivalent of one tablespoon.

Beans and Peas

Most but not all recipes give directions for cooking these and most varieties are available in cans. I always feel sad that delicatessen counters do not carry ready-cooked beans. The reason given is that demand would be too small so that wastage would be considerable since cooked beans do not keep well.

Cooked pulses keep very well in the freezer for at least two months provided they are not soft and mushy when frozen. Store them in boxes rather than bags. Since the shops do not provide this service it is a question of doing it yourself. Some beans, including red kidney beans and all those with thick shiny skins, may be toxic if incorrectly cooked. Aduki beans, lentils, chick peas and mung beans are excluded from this list.

In order to be sure that the beans will not cause upset tummies, soak them for at least five hours, then cook them in a full rolling boil for ten minutes before reducing the heat to complete the cooking. Use a large saucepan or pressure cooker which is ideal as temperatures reach in excess of boiling point. I do not recommend either the microwave or the slow cooker for the initial cooking period although you can finish the cooking in them.

You can halve the time needed for soaking by putting the beans in a saucepan and covering with plenty of cold water. Bring to the boil and leave in this water for two to three hours. After soaking rinse the beans and cook in fresh water. Do not add salt to the water as this toughens the skins.

Black-eye beans
Butter beans
Borlotti beans
Chick peas
Flageolet beans
Haricot beans
Lima beans
Rose cocoa beans
Pinto beans
Soya beans
Whole peas

The beans listed on the left must be pre-soaked. Cook them in four times their dry volume of water, measuring in cups if you find it more convenient (allow about 2 pints/1.1 litres water for each 8 oz/225g beans which will provide three to four servings on average). A teaspoon of oil added to the pot will reduce foaming. After fast boiling for an initial ten minutes, reduce the heat and simmer covered until the beans are tender.

Cooking times vary but on average take one to one and a half hours with the exception of chick peas which take one and a half to two hours and soya beans which take two and a half to three hours.

Split lentils and split peas need not be pre-soaked, although it would speed the cooking time. Lentils also cook well in the microwave. They will take twenty to thirty minutes cooked this way and thirty to forty minutes conventionally. Whole lentils benefit from a soak and take about one hour afterwards to cook.

In the pressure cooker split peas and lentils will take about fifteen minutes and with the exception of soya beans which take approximately forty minutes, most beans will take about twenty-five minutes. Follow the manufacturer's directions, but as a rule leave the trivet in position, add two pints of water for each pound of beans and do not cover until you have spooned away the scum.

Thaw and reheat frozen beans in a pan of boiling water, cooking for two to three minutes, and then rinse in cold water if they are required for salads. To use the microwave for thawing and reheating regenerate on full power in a covered dish, shaking it frequently. Take care when uncovering as overcooked beans may pop.

Rice freezes so well that I suggest you cook a really large amount and then freeze in suitable portions. Thaw and reheat any type of cooked rice in a pan of boiling water, in a steamer or in the microwave which is always a 100 per cent success and takes two to three minutes only.

Cook rice in a saucepan, in the pressure cooker, the slow cooker or steamer or bake in a lidded casserole in a moderate oven for 45 minutes to one hour. The microwave gives a wonderful performance with rice cookery. Follow the directions on the packet; 1 lb/455g long-grain rice will take about fifteen minutes on full power plus a five-minute standing time. For every 4 oz/115g brown rice you will need 1 pint/570ml hot water and ½ teaspoon salt. Cook covered on full power for twenty to twenty-five minutes, then switch off the current and leave the dish to stand for five minutes before fluffing up.

Cereals can be cooked with prior soaking or be frozen with ease with the exception of bulgur (cracked wheat) which requires only a ten-minute hot soak. Most other cereals are cooked in water for twenty to twenty-five minutes. Wholewheat can take up to one hour. The flavour of roast buckwheat is even further improved if it is lightly toasted before cooking. Thaw and reheat in a strainer over a pan of boiling water or in the microwave similarly to rice.

Sprouting

Sprouting is much easier to do than many people imagine. You must plan a few days ahead as it takes at least three days before shoots appear and growth will not continue after six days. Treat sprouted beans as you would mustard and cress or shop-bought beansprouts. They do not keep for very long so do not sprout more than you think you will need. A few tablespoons is sufficient for a four-portion serving.

There are various recommended methods of sprouting and if you are really keen a three-tiered sprouting pot is worth buying. Apart from this the best method is without doubt the jam jar. Any glass or pottery jar will do and the bigger the better. You will also need a large elastic band and a piece of porous material — ideally muslin or a 'J-cloth'. Pick over the beans to make sure there are no stones or grit and rinse in plenty of cold water. Put no more than a 1 inch/2.5cm depth of beans in a clean jar. Cover with the muslin and secure with the elastic band.

Fill the jar with water — cover with a lid or foil to prevent dust from entering and leave overnight until the beans are swollen to double their original size. Drain, refill the jar with cold water and then drain and repeat twice. Finally drain thoroughly, then put the jar on its side in a dish or on the draining board. Once or twice a day rinse the jar, drain well and replace the jar on its side. It is important to keep the jar in an airy place to avoid rancidity.

You can, if you prefer, sprout beans in a large strainer. You must carry out the initial twelve-hour soak in a bowl, then drain through the strainer. Leave the beans in the strainer placed on a plate to catch any drips and keep covered with a clean cloth. Rinse and drain every few hours and stir to prevent the beans sticking together.

By mistake I left some unsprouted soaked aduki beans in a strainer over the weekend. I reurned to find a ready grown salad for supper.

Refreshing Walnuts

Unless freshly shelled, walnuts tend to taste bitter. They can be freshened to recover that straight-off-the-tree taste in the following way. Put the shelled nuts in a small saucepan. Cover them with cold water, bring to the boil, drain and rinse in cold water. Repeat twice. After the final rinsing put the nuts in a small jug or bowl, cover with freshly drawn water and chill in the freezer for thirty minutes or overnight in the refrigerator. Drain and use as required. Refreshed walnuts can be stored only in the freezer but they are so more-ish that you will probably eat them all at once.

Unrefreshed nuts of all types store well in the freezer. Most will keep in the refrigerator for some time but salted peanuts (which are really a pulse) become stale after a week or so. Walnuts can also be refreshed in the microwave.

To roast or toast shelled hazelnuts or whole almonds spread the nuts out on a baking tray and put into a moderate oven or under the grill, stirring them occasionally until the skins are brittle. Toss the nuts in a clean teacloth to rub off the skins, then return the nuts to the heat for a few moments. Hazelnuts can be roasted in the microwave — you may find that a few burn in the centre. When cool store whole or grated in a screw-top jar or in the freezer.

To blanch nuts put them in a pan of water and bring to the boil. Leave for five minutes, then remove the skins.

Garnishing and Decorating

Well presented, well garnished food can transform an otherwise ordinary dish. A sprig of parsley or a slice of lemon is better than nothing. Two or three tiny sprigs of parsley or a fan of three thinly cut half lemon slices are even better. It is the delicate touch that sets off a dish. Apart from slices, half slices and wedges, lemon garnish can be a twist or butterfly. For either a thin centre slice is essential.

To make a twist make one cut from the edge to the centre. To make sure the garnish stays upright the cut edges must be twisted in opposite directions.

To make a butterfly, make 4 equidistant nicks through the peel only, then using a sharp knife cut away 2 opposite triangles to leave an hour glass shape.

Garnish with peeled, thinly sliced cucumber when a colour contrast is not desirable, sliced cucumber without peeling for a more contrasting effect. Alternate overlapping slices of each is one idea you may not have thought of. Use a cannelle knife to cut equidistant long strips of peel down the length of the cucumber and the resulting slices will resemble petals.

Use a sprinkling of chopped chives or better still a lattice of whole chives arranged on a pie or gratin. A novel way of using chives is to plait them, then blanch in hot water so that they will not unravel.

To make radish flowers make four deep cuts around the radishes, then four smaller cuts lower down. Soak in ice-cold water in the refrigerator until the petals open out.

Celery sticks cut into 3 inch/7.5cm lengths and then pared thinly with a potato peeler will curl after being submerged in ice-cold water for a few hours.

Trim spring onions, cutting away most of the green part and make several 2 inch/5cm long cuts along either end. They will open out and curl over like Chinese fans after similar soaking.

Use a cannelle knife or a sharp stainless steel kitchen knife to fashion carrot daisies. Cut well-scraped, even-sized carrots into 2 inch/5cm lengths and make 'V' shaped channels at intervals down the length. Cut carrots into thin slices and blanch in boiling water before giving them a cold soak. Carrots that are insufficiently scraped will blacken around the edges.

Button mushrooms should be thinly sliced and dipped in lemon juice before using as a garnish and whole button mushrooms look beautiful when 'tooled' with a cannelle knife.

Tomato skin roses are pretty but if you haven't made them before allow some time for practice. Thinly peel in a spiral fashion, then pare the flesh from the skin around the edges and roll up tightly — plant into soft sauced dishes.

Desserts are easier to decorate, the garnish usually consisting of one of the reserved ingredients such as cherries or strawberries. Toasted nuts of all kinds, angelica leaves, glacé cherries and the like may not seem very exotic but do the job well enough. Piped whipped cream rosettes or scrolls look marvellous if they are well done.

Chocolate caraque, finely grated chocolate, chocolate run-outs (when a design is piped or spread on non-stick paper to be removed after setting) are all variations for decorations and marzipan leaves and flowers are great fun to make.

Haute cuisiniers will spend time cooking syrup and spinning it to form a brittle web and although many think it 'twee' there is no doubt that a single fresh rose-bud complete with leaves placed on the side of the plate is a sign of elegant decadence.

Barbecue Sauce _____Makes about ½ pint/285ml

Serve with hot cutlets, lentil patties or similar dry foods or to enliven most pasta and rice dishes.

2 shallots
2 celery sticks
1 tablespoon sunflower oil
3 tablespoons red wine vinegar
3 tablespoons tomato purée
1 tablespoon Holbrook's sauce
1 tablespoon fresh lemon juice
1 × 14 oz/400g tin chopped tomatoes
½ pint/285ml vegetable stock
Few sprigs parsley
Few sprigs thyme
½ teaspoon bay leaf powder
Sea salt
Freshly milled black pepper

1 Peel and finely chop the shallots. Finely slice the celery. Fry in the oil, stirring frequently over moderate heat until soft.

2 Add all the remaining ingredients, bring to the boil, then simmer uncovered, stirring occasionally, for 30 minutes or until the sauce thickens. Season with salt and pepper.

3 Liquidize or purée the sauce by pressing through a sieve.

4 Store in a jar, covered with a jam-pot cover and screw-top lid.

Beurre Manié

Beurre manié is a valuable thickening agent. Whisk tiny amounts into bubbling hot liquids to thicken and form a sauce. Add to liquid in which vegetables have been cooked or milk to make a quick white sauce. Basic white sauces can be frozen but need a lot of beating to make them smooth and I believe the beurre manié method is better.

Butter
Flour
To prepare, blend butter and flour together in the proportion of three to two, i.e. 6 oz/170g flour to 4 oz/115g butter. Freeze in balls or measured amounts.

To make half a pint of coating sauce, heat ½ pint milk until it begins to rise up the side of the pan. Whisk in 5×½ oz/15g pats of beurre manié one at a time and cook for thirty seconds.

For a savoury sauce season with salt and pepper, herbs and mustard powder or grated cheese. For a sweet sauce add honey or syrup, grated chocolate or mashed banana. Serve hot.

Brown Rolls

I use 81% wheatmeal flour to make these rolls because I find them
lighter than when using 100% wholemeal flour.

*1 lb/455g 81% wheatmeal
flour
1 teaspoon salt
1 × ¼ oz/6g sachet easy blend
dried yeast
1 oz/30g soft margarine
About ¾ pint/425ml warm
water
Milk or beaten egg*

1 Put the flour, salt and yeast in a mixing bowl and
rub in the margarine. Pour in sufficient water to mix
to a very soft dough (do not add extra flour as the
bran present in the flour continues to absorb
moisture during rising).
2 Leave for 10 minutes, then turn on to a lightly
floured worktop and knead until smooth. Divide the
dough into fifteen even pieces and shape into rolls
with a cupped hand on a lightly greased surface.
3 Space out the uncooked rolls on a well-greased
baking tray and cover with greased polythene, greased
side against the rolls. Leave in a warm kitchen until
doubled in size. Brush the tops of the rolls with milk
or beaten egg if desired.
4 Preheat the oven to 450°F/230°C/Gas Mark 8 and
bake for 10 to 15 minutes until the rolls are crisp and
sound hollow when tapped sharply underneath.
Serve warm or leave to cool and freeze. Reheat from
frozen in a hot oven for 5 minutes.

Classic Mayonnaise _____Makes about 7 fl oz/200ml

One of the reasons that mayonnaise curdles is that the egg yolk is
not sufficiently warm when the room temperature oil and vinegar
are blended; the only way to warm the egg yolk is to beat
vigorously with the seasonings before the liquids are added. If you
are making this mayonnaise by hand you are likely to be successful
using just one egg yolk, but when a hand-held or electric whisk is
used the depth of egg yolk in the bowl may be insufficient to be
beaten thoroughly.

1-2 egg yolks
Pinch mustard powder
Pinch sea salt
Pinch freshly ground black
pepper
¼ pint/140ml sunflower oil
1-2 tablespoons vinegar or
lemon juice

1 Put the egg yolk and seasonings in a bowl and beat
thoroughly with a wooden spoon or whisk until
fluffy. Gradually beat in the oil drop by drop, stirring
all the time, until the mixture is thick. Do not add
more oil than is necessary as one egg yolk cannot
incorporate more than ¼ pint/140ml oil, after which
the mayonnaise would curdle.
2 Gradually beat in the vinegar or lemon juice and if
the mayonnaise is too thick add 1-2 teaspoons warm
water. Store in a bottle or jar in the refrigerator.
Makes about 7 fl oz/200ml and will keep in the
refrigerator for one week. Do not freeze.

For variations add chopped parsley or chives which
gives a good flavour and pretty green effect. Add 1
teaspoon mild curry base (see page 32 or 33), or mix
the mayonnaise with a little tomato purée and
Holbrook's sauce to form a cocktail base for
shredded vegetables.

Cold Sauce Tartare
_____Makes about ¼ pint/140ml

¼ pint/140ml thick
mayonnaise (see page 29)
3 cocktail gherkins
2 spring onions
2 teaspoons chopped capers
2 teaspoons chopped chives
1 tablespoon freshly chopped
parsley
Sea salt
Freshly ground black pepper

1 Put the mayonnaise into a bowl, then finely chop and add the gherkins, trim and finely slice the spring onions, then mix in the capers, chives and parsley.
2 Season with salt and pepper and serve with nut cutlets or tomato salad. Makes ¼ pint/140ml and will keep in the refrigerator for up to one week. Do not freeze.

Croûtons _____

Croûtons absorb a large amount of oil so use more than you think is needed. If the bread absorbs all the oil in the pan and the croûtons are not cooked, add more oil a little at a time so that the temperature is not drastically reduced.

Day-old wholemeal bread
Sunflower oil

1 Cut the bread into ½ inch/1cm slices.
2 Remove the crusts and dice the bread into ½ inch/1cm squares.
3 Heat about 4 tablespoons oil until a bread cube browns after 20 seconds, then add a handful of bread cubes, tossing them with a fish slice to brown all sides. Remove and drain on kitchen paper.
4 Add and heat more oil if needed and fry bread cubes in further batches.
5 Store croûtons in an airtight container in the refrigerator or freezer.

Variations:

Garlic Croûtons

Rub the pan generously with garlic before frying and squeeze garlic juice or garlic salt on to the bread before dicing.

Paprika Croûtons

Add 1 teaspoon paprika to the oil before heating, adding a little more between each batch.

Parmesan Croûtons

Toss fried croûtons in Parmesan cheese while still hot.

Crumble Mix

This is used for a topping on savoury casseroles and fruit puddings. Make up a large batch and use as required. A fruit crumble will take about 30 minutes in a fairly hot oven, 400°F/200°C/Gas Mark 6, and with savoury crumbles add the topping towards the end of cooking the filling and allow about 20 minutes afterwards. Store in a well-sealed freezer bag. Crumble mix can be used directly from the freezer and needs no prior thawing. A crumble mix is simply a dry pastry mix.

6 oz/170g wholemeal flour
2 oz/55g self-raising flour
4 oz/115g butter or *margarine*

Crumble Mix 1

Mix the flours together. Cut up and rub in the butter until the mixture resembles fine crumbs.

6 oz/170g wholemeal flour
4 oz/115g butter or *margarine*
1 oz/30g porridge oats
1 oz/30g chopped mixed nuts

Crumble Mix 2

Put the flour in a mixing bowl and rub in the butter until the mixture resembles coarse breadcrumbs. Stir in the oats and nuts.

To either of these crumble mixtures add 2-3 oz/55-85g demerara sugar and sweet spices for sweet crumble toppings, salt, freshly-milled black pepper and 1-2 teaspoons herbs for savoury toppings.

Curry Base _____ Takes about 20 minutes

Curry pastes in varying strengths are now widely available. They
are meant to impregnate the food and each has its own distinct
taste. Store these curry bases in plastic-lidded jars in a cool larder.
For longer storage, freeze well wrapped in suitable portions. Use
them for quick cook or prepare ahead curries whenever you wish.
Each recipe makes ¾ pint/425ml of mild curry base. For medium
hot increase the chilli powder to 2 teaspoons. For most recipes
serving four you will need about ¼ pint/140ml.

1 whole garlic bulb
3 large onions
¼ pint/140ml sunflower oil
½ pint/285ml thick-set
natural yogurt (not
home-made)
1 teaspoon cornflour
6 tablespoons ground cumin
6 tablespoons ground coriander
1 teaspoon turmeric
1½ teaspoons chilli powder
1 teaspoon sea salt

Muglai Curry Base

1 Peel and chop the garlic cloves (about 12) and set
aside. Peel and finely chop the onions.
2 Heat the oil in a preferably non-stick frying-pan or
heavy-based saucepan and when hot fry the onions
until just beginning to brown. Add the garlic and fry
until completely brown.
3 While the onion and garlic are frying, blend
together the yogurt, cornflour, cumin, coriander,
turmeric, chilli powder and salt.
4 Reduce the heat under the frying-pan and
gradually add the yogurt, blending a tablespoon at a
time, stirring frequently. If the mixture sticks to the
bottom of the pan add a little water.
5 Simmer for 3-5 minutes until just boiling, then
remove from the heat and drain off the excess oil if to
be used immediately.

Opposite *Gaspacho (page 54) and Celery and Blue Cheese
Soup (page 52).*

Whole Spice Curry Base

3 large onions
1 whole bulb garlic
¼ pint/140ml sunflower oil
1 tablespoon cumin seeds
1 tablespoon mustard seeds
12 black peppercorns
16 whole green cardamoms
4 tablespoons tomato purée
2 bay leaves
¼ teaspoon ground cloves
1½ teaspoons chilli powder
2 tablespoons ground cumin
2 tablespoons ground coriander
3×1 inch/2.5cm pieces cinnamon stick
1½ teaspoons sea salt
About ¼ pint/140ml hot water

1 Peel and chop the onions and garlic separately.
2 Heat the oil in a deep heavy-based saucepan. Add the cumin, mustard seeds, peppercorns and cardamoms and fry briskly until the seeds begin to pop.
3 Add the onions and fry until they begin to brown, then stir in the garlic and continue frying until golden.
4 Stir in the tomato purée, bay leaves, ground cloves, chilli powder, ground cumin, ground coriander, cinnamon stick, salt and hot water.
5 Simmer gently uncovered for 20-30 minutes, stirring occasionally, until thick. Cover and leave to cool. Remove the bay leaves and cinnamon stick. Drain off the surplus oil.

Dhal _____Serves 5-7

Dhal freezes well but water or stock will be needed in thawing and reheating. Serve with curries or spicy dishes or omit the spices and curry powders from the ingredients for a blander vegetable accompaniment.

8 oz/225g yellow split peas
1¼ pints/710ml vegetable stock or water
1 teaspoon turmeric
½ teaspoon ground ginger
1 tablespoon garam masala
2 bay leaves
1 large onion
1 garlic clove
2-3 tablespoons sunflower oil
Sea salt
Freshly ground black pepper

1 Rinse the split peas and put in a heavy-based saucepan with the stock or water. Bring to the boil, then simmer uncovered for 30 minutes, spooning away the scum as it forms.
2 Stir in the turmeric and ginger, garam masala and bay leaves and continue cooking for 30 minutes or until all the liquid is absorbed.
3 While the split peas are cooking peel and chop the onion and crush the garlic. Fry in the oil until crisp. Drain on kitchen paper.
4 Remove the bay leaves. Mash the split peas. Season with salt and pepper and stir in half the onions.
5 Serve in a heated bowl and garnish with the remaining fried onions.

Opposite *Tahini Dip (page 61); Hummus (page 56); and Pineapple and Walnut Pâté (page 60).*

Flour Tortillas _____Makes 12

Flour tortillas can be cooked ahead and stored well wrapped in foil
in the freezer. Reheat briefly in the microwave or frying-pan or grill.
Use with Mexican dishes or in place of pitta, chapattis or nan.

6 oz/170g plain flour
2 oz/55g wholemeal flour
1 teaspoon sea salt
2 oz/55g white vegetable fat
6–8 tablespoons warm water

1 Mix the flours and salt in a mixing bowl. Add the fat and mix with a fork.
2 Gradually add the water, kneading to a soft, slightly moist dough. Wrap and set aside for 30 minutes.
3 Divide the dough into twelve pieces. With floured hands shape into balls, then roll out on plenty of flour to thin pancakes. Use an upturned plate to trim to an even shape.
4 Heat an ungreased frying-pan and cook the tortillas for 20 seconds on each side or until brown patches appear.
5 Store between non-stick baking parchment discs and wrap in a dry teacloth.

French Dressing _____Makes about ¼ pint/140ml

This is a piquant dressing often used with avocados.

6 tablespoons sunflower oil
3 tablespoons white wine vinegar
6 tablespoons freshly chopped parsley
1 tablespoon French mustard
½ teaspoon light soft brown sugar
½ teaspoon sea salt
¼ teaspoon freshly ground black pepper

1 Mix the oil and vinegar together, then gradually stir in the remaining ingredients.
2 Store in a screw-top jar with a plastic lid or in a well-corked, wide-necked bottle in a cool place. Shake well before serving.

Hollandaise Sauce _____Makes about ¼ pint/140ml

Contrary to popular belief Hollandaise sauce will in fact freeze.
There are several methods and a few variations on the ingredients
but this is one that you might like to try.

1 tablespoon tarragon vinegar
2 tablespoons cold water
2 egg yolks
2 oz/55g butter
1 tablespoon fresh lemon juice
Sea salt
White pepper

1 Put the vinegar, water and egg yolks in a medium bowl and beat thoroughly together.
2 Place the bowl over a saucepan containing about 1 inch/2.5cm hot water and place over minimum heat. Cook the sauce, whisking continuously until it thickens, then remove the pan from the heat.
3 Add the butter to the sauce in small pieces, beating in between each addition. Stir in the lemon juice, season to taste with salt and pepper and serve warm.

Herb Butter _____

Herb butter adds a gourmet touch and can be made with hard
margarine instead. Simply beat about 4 oz/115g butter with a little
lemon juice and 5-6 tablespoons finely chopped herbs, adding salt
and pepper to taste.

When the mixture is thoroughly blended place on greaseproof paper and shape into a 'sausage' about 1 inch/2.5cm thick. Roll up the butter in the greaseproof paper and twist the ends cracker fashion. Overwrap with foil and store in the freezer. Remove from the freezer about fifteen minutes before using, slice thinly and then refrigerate.

Herb butter can be shaped in various ways, one of which is to form balls with a potato baller and then open freeze. Place them when frozen in a sealed box and store in the freezer. They can be taken straight from the freezer for use on hot dishes.

Home-baked Crisps

These are so delicious that they can be served as nibbles, as a garnish, as a topping or with dips. After cooking store in an airtight container, preferably in the freezer. Wrap a tablespoon of raw rice in a sheet of kitchen paper or small piece of muslin and put into the bottom of the box to help keep the crisps crisp.

Crisps are quick to prepare if you have a food processor fitted with a slicing disc or a mandoline or a grater with a grating blade. Otherwise slice thinly with a sharp knife or pare with a wide-bladed potato peeler.

4 tablespoons sunflower oil
2 lb/900g potatoes
Sea salt

1 Prepare a fairly hot oven 400°F/200°C/Gas Mark 6.

2 Put the oil in a large shallow dish and set aside.

3 Peel the potatoes and slice wafer thin. Rinse in several changes of cold water and dry in a clean teacloth. Toss the slices in the oil, making sure that they are all well coated. Season with salt.

4 Spread the potato slices out in a single layer on large baking trays and bake for 20-25 minutes until golden brown. Some slices will brown more quickly than others. Remove these as soon as they are cooked.

N.B. The crisps will stick to the baking tray only if they are insufficiently cooked or overcooked.

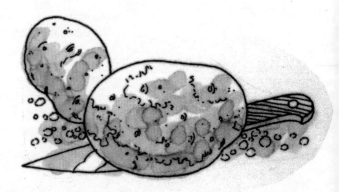

Irish Soda Bread

¾ lb/800g wholemeal flour
1 pint/570ml milk
1 teaspoon sea salt
4 tablespoons baking powder
1½ oz/40g soft margarine
3 tablespoons molasses

1 Mix half the flour with all of the milk. Beat thoroughly, cover and set aside in a warm place for 30-45 minutes.
2 Mix the remaining flour, salt and baking powder together and stir in the margarine and molasses.
3 Heat the oven to 425°F/225°C/Gas Mark 7.
4 Beat the batter into the dough until well mixed. Shape into a 5 inch/12.5cm round on a floured surface and place on a well-greased baking tray. Cut a deep cross through the dough.
5 Bake for 30-45 minutes or until the bottom of the loaf sounds hollow when tapped. Eat fresh or freeze whole or in four sections.

Light Mayonnaise _____Makes ½ pint/285ml

This mayonnaise must be made in the liquidizer. A whole egg is used to produce a light fluffy texture.

1 egg
Pinch mustard powder
¼ teaspoon sea salt
¼ teaspoon white pepper
1 tablespoon white wine vinegar
½ pint/285ml sunflower oil

1 Break the egg into the liquidizer goblet, add the mustard powder, salt, pepper and vinegar and switch on at high speed until the mixture is well blended and fluffy.
2 Switch on the liquidizer to its highest speed and pour in the oil through the aperture in a thin but steady stream and do not switch off until the mayonnaise thickens. You may see a slight oily patch on top of the mayonnaise but this can be mixed in by hand when the mayonnaise is spooned into a jar. The recipe makes ½ pint/285ml and will keep in the refrigerator for one week.

Melba Toast

Allow an uninterrupted half hour to make Melba toast. The splitting has to be done when the toast is hot. Remove curled toast with a tong and spread on kitchen paper to avoid softening. Thick slices cut from a 'sandwich' loaf or medium thick ready-sliced bread are best.

1 Lightly toast the bread on both sides. Remove the crust.

2 While still hot lay the toast on a chopping board. Rest the palm of a hand on the toast and using a sharp knife cut through horizontally to within ¼ inch/5mm of one edge.

3 Without withdrawing the knife place the toast vertically on the board and press the knife handle so that the blade separates the halves. There will now be two wafer-thin pieces toasted only on one side.

4 Halve these diagonally and toast the uncooked side until the corners curl up.

5 Use within a few hours or store in an airtight container in the freezer if you wish. Crisp in a hot oven before serving.

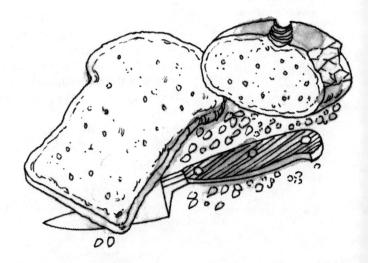

Microwaved Hollandaise Sauce _____ Makes ½ pint/285ml

When Hollandaise is made in the microwave the sequence and
method are totally different from when conventionally cooked.

5 oz/150g unsalted butter
2 tablespoons fresh lemon juice
¼ pint/140ml double cream
2 egg yolks, at room
temperature
½ teaspoon sea salt
¼ teaspoon white pepper
1 extra teaspoon butter

1 Put the butter into a medium bowl and heat on
full power until melted and clear, about 1 minute.
Whisk in the lemon juice, cream, egg yolks, salt and
pepper and at this stage the mixture will appear to
thicken.

2 Cook on full power, whisking every 15 seconds,
until the sauce thickens, about 1 minute in all.
During the first stages of cooking the sauce will
become very thin but subsequently will thicken up. If
you overcook and the sauce begins to curdle around
the edges remove from the microwave and beat
vigorously.

3 When the sauce is cooked remove from the
microwave and continue whisking until frothy, then
beat in the teaspoon of butter.

4 Makes ½ pint/285ml and can be frozen in an
airtight container after cooling. To regenerate,
unmould the block of Hollandaise sauce into a small
bowl and heat gently on the defrost setting, beating
with a fork as soon as the block begins to thaw
around the edges.

Pastry

Keep a baked pastry case or two in an airtight tin for a week or two
or well-wrapped in the freezer for a month. Use commercial
shortcrust made with vegetable fat or make up your own.
Do not refreeze previously thawed pastry and do not keep rolled-
out raw pastry at room temperature or in the refrigerator for more
than a few hours or it will develop little black specks, indicating
that it has gone mouldy. Freshly made pastry can be frozen but it
does mean the temporary loss of the dish while in the freezer.
Here are two recipes for wholemeal pastry. The secret is to allow a
standing time before rolling and the pastry must be very thin. Bake
in a fairly hot oven for 25–30 minutes. If after baking blind the
pastry is filled and baked further to cook the filling, the oven
temperature must then be reduced.

5 oz/140g wholemeal flour
Pinch sea salt
3 oz/85g solid vegetable
cooking fat
About 2 tablespoons cold
water

1 Put the flour and salt in a mixing bowl. Add the
fat and using two table knives chop and mix with the
flour until the mixture resembles hazelnut-sized
crumbs. Stir in the water and knead lightly. Leave to
stand for ten minutes.
2 Roll out thinly on a lightly floured surface. Ignore
any small patches of white fat that may show
through. Add a little extra flour to prevent the pastry
from sticking to the rolling pin.
3 Fit into a lightly-greased, loose-bottomed 8
inch/20cm flan tin. Prick the base thoroughly and
bake blind (i.e. line with greaseproof paper and baking
beans) for 15 minutes.
4 Remove the paper and beans and bake for a
further 10–15 minutes. Leave to cool, then overwrap
and freeze.

3 oz/85g wholemeal flour
3 oz/85g 81% wheatmeal
flour
1½ oz/40g butter
1½ oz/40g solid vegetable fat
About 2 tablespoons cold
water

For a lighter pastry use:

1 Mix the flours in a large bowl and rub in the
butter and fat until the mixture resembles
breadcrumbs. Mix in sufficient water to make a soft
dough.
2 Leave to stand for 10 minutes before rolling out,
then continue as in the previous recipe.

Pesto

It is worth making your own pesto which I think is superior to the
bottled kind, but it does require fresh basil. Use pesto with pasta,
rice or to enliven a simple white sauce.

3 oz/85g fresh basil leaves
1 clove garlic
¼ teaspoon sea salt
2 oz/55g pine nuts
6 tablespoons olive oil
½ teaspoon freshly ground
black pepper
1½ oz/40g grated Sardo
cheese

Either:

Chop the basil leaves, crush the garlic and put in a
mortar with the salt and pine nuts, pound with a
pestle or the end of a rolling pin, then beat in the oil
a little at a time, season with pepper and stir in the
cheese.

Or:

Purée all the ingredients except the cheese in the
liquidizer, then stir in the cheese. Pour into a jar
covered with a wax disc and screw-top lid and store in
the refrigerator for up to one month.

Pimiento and Tomato Sauce

A cook ahead sauce which can be deep frozen. It does not keep for
more than a day or two under refrigeration. Serve with pasta and
rice dishes.

1 small onion
Oil for frying
14 oz/400g tin pimientos
14 oz/400g tin chopped
tomatoes
1 tablespoon vodka
¼ pint/140ml red wine
3 tablespoons tomato paste
1 teaspoon dried basil
1 teaspoon soft dark brown
sugar
Sea salt
Freshly ground black pepper

1 Peel and finely chop the onion and sauté in the oil
in a heavy-based saucepan until the onion is soft.
2 Drain the pimientos and add to the pan with all
the remaining ingredients.
3 Bring to the boil, reduce the heat and simmer,
stirring occasionally, until the sauce thickens.
4 Press through a sieve or purée in the liquidizer.
Adjust the seasoning. After cooking freeze in suitable
amounts.

Raita

Take care when chopping fresh chilli as the juices can burn
the lips and make the eyes smart. If you wish to cheat use a pinch of
chilli powder.

8 fl oz/225ml natural thick
yogurt
½ teaspoon cumin seeds
½ teaspoon sea salt
½ teaspoon freshly ground
black pepper
1 medium onion
½ green chilli
½ large cucumber

1 Put the yogurt into a mixing bowl and beat until
smooth. Stir in the cumin, salt and pepper.
2 Peel and finely slice the onions and separate into
rings. Blanch, de-seed and finely chop the chilli. Peel
and dice the cucumber.
3 Mix the cucumber, onions and chilli into the
yogurt, cover and chill in the refrigerator for at least 1
hour.

Salad Cream _____ Makes about ½ pint/285ml

This recipe has better keeping qualities than mayonnaise because
the egg is cooked. There is less likelihood of curdling and you do
not need a whisk to prepare the sauce.

1 tablespoon plain flour
1 tablespoon caster sugar
1 teaspoon sea salt
1 teaspoon mustard powder
3 tablespoons fresh lemon juice
5 tablespoons cold water
½ oz/15g butter
1 egg
4 tablespoons single cream

1 Blend the flour, sugar, salt and mustard powder
together in a small saucepan. Then stir in the lemon
juice and water. Put the saucepan over low heat and
cook the sauce for 5 minutes, stirring all the time.
2 Stir in the butter and cook for a further 20-30
seconds or until nearly boiling. Draw the pan away
from the heat.
3 Beat the egg with 2 tablespoons of the hot sauce,
pour back into the saucepan and beat thoroughly.
Pour into a warm jar and leave until cold, then cover
with the lid and refrigerate.
4 Stir the cream into the sauce just before serving.
Makes about ½ pint/285ml and will keep in the
refrigerator for 1-2 weeks. Do not freeze.

Sautéed Onion Purée _____Makes about 1 lb/455g

So many recipes call for sautéed onions that I thought it would be a
good idea to do these in advance and store them in the freezer to be
ready to use to perk up a soup or to start off a vegetable recipe. If
you have a food processor you can make up a huge quantity and
the purée will keep in the refrigerator for up to about four weeks or
in the freezer for 2-3 months. Freeze the sautéed onion in small
quantities as it is not easy to break a piece off immediately it is
required.

1 lb/455g onions
4 oz/115g butter or margarine

1 Peel the onions and slice as thinly as possible. Put
the butter or margarine into a large heavy-based
saucepan and fry gently for about 10 minutes or until
they are golden brown.
2 Remove the pan from the heat and leave the
onions to cool in the butter. Either freeze at this stage
or purée in the food processor or liquidizer. Store in
small boxes or jars, covered and overwrapped to
prevent the odour from affecting other stored
ingredients.

Thick Tomato Sauce _____Makes ¾ pint/425ml

Serve with pasta or vegetables. A useful recipe to prepare when
tomatoes are cheap and plentiful. I do not advocate removing the
tomato skins as I feel it is a waste of useful fibre in the diet.

1 lb/455g ripe tomatoes
2 garlic cloves
¼ teaspoon sea salt
1 tablespoon olive oil
½ teaspoon dried marjoram
1 tablespoon freshly chopped
parsley
Freshly ground black pepper

1 Chop the tomatoes.
2 Peel and crush the garlic with the salt.
3 Heat the oil, add the garlic and sauté for a minute
or two. Add the tomatoes, marjoram and parsley and
cook, stirring continuously, until the tomatoes are
soft. Season with the pepper.
4 Mash with a potato masher or purée in the
liquidizer.

Vinaigrette _____Makes about ¼ pint/140ml

Vinaigrette is sometimes described as French dressing but
vinaigrette has only salt and pepper to flavour it. Thus good quality
olive oil and wine or cider vinegar are essential. Your choice of red
or white wine vinegar depends upon the ingredients the vinaigrette
is being mixed with; pale salads look better when white wine
vinegar is used. Either mix in a wide-necked screw-topped jar or in
a measuring jug as it is extremely difficult to pour directly into a
bottle without everything spilling all over the place. The usual
proportions are 3 tablespoons oil to 1 tablespoon vinegar but this
can be adjusted according to individual taste. To create herb
dressings such as tarragon, thyme or garlic, simply add fresh herbs
or cloves of garlic to the vinaigrette and leave them to permeate the
dressing.

6 tablespoons olive oil
2 tablespoons wine or *cider*
vinegar
½ teaspoon sea salt
¼ teaspoon freshly ground
black pepper

1 Mix all the ingredients together in a jar. Cover
with a well-fitting screw-top plastic lid and keep in a
cool place. Shake well before using.
2 This quantity makes about ¼ pint/140ml but the
quantity can be increased as the vinaigrette keeps very
well indeed.

4 Starters

The starter sets the tone for the meal. It must above all be neat and attractive. Many starters can be pre-prepared and arranged prettily garnished on individual dishes or plates or in glasses. Try to use utensils that complement the food.

Colour is more important than shape. The dish should blend in or contrast with the food; cold food looks better on white, cream, pink or green backgrounds; hot food will look warming in deep browns and reds. There is nothing to compare with clear glass to show off a layered recipe. If a tureen of hot soup is being brought to the table, leave the lid in place until all your guests are seated. Uncover and await appreciative murmurs as the aroma escapes. A touch of showmanship without being obviously pretentious will put your guests into the right frame of mind, eager to enjoy what you are putting before them.

Some of the starters in this chapter are also suitable to be served as main courses and these are marked with an asterisk. They would normally serve two but the quantities can be increased or alternatively two or three different vegetable-based starters can be substituted, presented on larger dishes and served at the table.

American Grapefruit

Allow plenty of time for preparation and you will be rewarded with
a rapturous reception.

2 large grapefruits
1 red apple
4 maraschino cherries

1 Halve the grapefruits across and loosen the
segments with a grapefruit knife.
2 Using scissors cut around the outside of the fruit
to sever the membranes.
3 Loosen the core underneath with the grapefruit
knife and pull out the membranes.
4 Using the scissors cut out a zig-zag pattern around
the rim of the skin. The fruit sinks a little after
preparation.
5 Rinse and dry the apple. Cut into quarters and
remove the core. Slice the apple quarters thinly and
cut each slice in half. Insert slices of apple skin-side up
between the grapefruit segments, pushing them in
firmly to avoid discoloration.
6 Serve topped with a cherry.

Artichauds au Citron Vert

Artichokes, although low in calories, become exceedingly fattening
when served with a butter sauce. By serving in the following way
guests may omit the butter if they wish.

4 globe artichokes
2 limes
2 oz/55g butter
Sea salt
Freshly ground black pepper

1 Wash the artichokes in cold salted water. Cut off
the stalks. Open out the leaves and cut away the tips.
Remove the inside choke with a sharp-edged spoon
or grapefruit knife.
2 Squeeze and reserve the juice from the limes. Insert
the shell halves open-side up into the artichoke
cavities to maintain their shape and give them
flavour.
3 Bring a large pan of water to the boil, put in the
artichokes, stalk-side underneath. Bring back to the
boil, then cover with a lid. Reduce the heat and
simmer for about 30 minutes or until a leaf can be
easily pulled away.

4 Drain upside-down — the lime shell should stay in place. Melt the butter and add the lime juice to taste. Season with salt and pepper. Pour into the lime shells.
5 Serve with large table napkins and individual dishes of cold water for guests to dip their fingers.

Asparagus with Yogurt and Chive Dressing

QC ★ Serves 4
Takes about 35 minutes

May and June are the best months for asparagus. Purchase the larger variety for this recipe.

1¾ lb/1kg fresh asparagus
Sea salt
1 tablespoon fresh lemon juice
Small knob butter
24 chives
¼ pint/140ml low-fat natural yogurt
Freshly ground black pepper

1 Scrape or lightly peel the asparagus stems and cut away the tough stalk end. Rinse in cold water.
2 Bring a large saucepan of salted water to the boil. Add the lemon juice and butter.
3 Layer the asparagus in the pan, reduce the heat and cover with a lid. Cook over low heat for about 20 minutes until the tips are tender. Drain.
4 Set aside 12 chives and chop the remainder. Mix with the yogurt and some black pepper.
5 Make four plaits with the chives, using 3 chives for each. Arrange a sheaf of asparagus on warm individual plates and wrap around the waist with a plait of chives (see pages 24-5). Pour a little of the sauce on one side of the plate.

Baked Potato Skins
with Dill Dunkers _____PA Serves 4-5

Use up the potato pulp to serve as mashed or duchesse potato in
another recipe.

4 baking potatoes
½ oz/15g butter
1 tablespoon grated Parmesan
8 oz/225g cottage cheese
1 tablespoon chopped chives
1 teaspoon chopped dill weed
Sea salt
Freshly ground black pepper
Sprigs dill weed, to garnish

Optional Advance Preparations

Up to 48 hours ahead

1 Scrub the potatoes, prick thoroughly and bake in a
very hot oven, 450°F/220°C/Gas Mark 7, for 45
minutes to 1 hour until cooked.

2 Halve the potatoes lengthwise, scoop out the pulp,
leaving a ¼ inch/5mm wall. Put a little butter inside
each skin and spread with a spoon. Sprinkle with
Parmesan.

3 Replace in the oven for 5 minutes or until crisp
inside. Cut into quarters with kitchen scissors. Leave
to cool. Store in an airtight container.

Up to 24 hours ahead

4 Beat the cottage cheese, chives and chopped dill
weed together and season with salt and pepper.
Refrigerate.

15 minutes before serving

5 Spread the potato skins out on a greased baking
sheet and place in a hot oven for 5 minutes.

To assemble

6 Put the sauce in a small bowl in the centre of a
serving platter. Garnish with dill sprigs. Arrange the
potato skins around the bowl.

Beetroot in Orange Vinaigrette

NC   Serves 4
Takes about 10 minutes

Raw beetroots are easy to cook and you have the advantage of
being able to choose just how tender you like them to be. Boil them
in their skins complete with stalks.

4 small cooked beetroots
4 spring onions
1 small orange
4 tablespoons safflower oil
Sea salt
Freshly ground black pepper
1 tablespoon roasted pumpkin
seeds
1 box alfalfa

1 Place the beetroots on a chopping board and
remove a thin slice from the bases if they will not
stand erect.

2 Make thin deep vertical slits across the beetroot
but do not cut through to the base.

3 Top, tail and finely slice the onions and place in
the slits in the beetroot.

4 Grate the orange zest and squeeze the juice. Mix
with the oil, season lightly with salt and pepper and
stir in the pumpkin seeds.

5 When ready to serve, arrange the beetroots on a
bed of alfalfa and pour over the vinaigrette.

Camembert Soufflé Glacé _____PA ★ Serves 4-8

This recipe can also be served as a main course with various salads or in a small quantity as an after-dinner savoury. To make cucumber twists, make sharp cuts from edge to centre of thin cucumber slices, then 'twist' so that the ends are facing in opposite directions.

1 oz/30g butter
1 oz/30g plain flour
½ pint/285ml milk
3 oz/85g Camembert
1 tablespoon tomato purée
1 tablespoon French mustard
¼ teaspoon paprika
2 eggs plus 1 extra egg white
1 tablespoon agar-agar

Optional Advance Preparations

Up to 24 hours ahead

1 Prepare 6-10 individual ramekin dishes. Make collars of double thickness greaseproof paper 1¼ times the circumference of the dish and about ½ inch/1cm taller than the dish. Tie under the rim so that there is no gap between the collar and the dish.
2 Melt the butter in a saucepan, then stir in the flour. Cook for 1 minute, stirring occasionally. Gradually mix in the milk and cook over moderate heat, stirring continuously until the sauce thickens. Cook for a further minute.
3 Remove the rind and mash the Camembert. Mix into the sauce, add the tomato purée, mustard and paprika.
4 Separate the eggs, beat the yolks with 2 tablespoons cold water and mix in the agar-agar.
5 Mix into the sauce and cook over low heat, stirring all the time until the sauce is very thick. Remove from the heat and leave to cool down, stirring frequently to prevent a skin forming.
6 With clean beaters, whip the egg whites until stiff. Fold into the warm sauce, pour into the ramekin dishes and refrigerate until set and cold.

To assemble

7 Separate the paper collar from the 'soufflés' with a warmed table knife. Decorate with cucumber twists.

Celery and Carrot Cream Slaw

NC   Serves 4
_____Takes about 15 minutes

Light mayonnaise is made with whole eggs rather than yolks only
and is less rich.

2 tablespoons soured cream
2 tablespoons Dijon mustard
4 tablespoons light mayonnaise
(see page 37)
4 celery stalks
6 oz/170g carrots
4 large lettuce leaves
1 tablespoon freshly chopped
parsley

1 Mix the soured cream, mustard and mayonnaise in a large bowl.
2 Very finely slice the celery, scrape and grate the carrots. Mix with the dressing.
3 Place a lettuce leaf on each individual plate. Pile the slaw on top. Garnish with the parsley.

Celery and Blue Cheese Soup_____PA Serves 4-6

The cheese adds extra flavour and gives this non-creamy soup a
touch of class.

1 head celery
1 medium onion
½ oz/15g butter
1 pint/570ml vegetable stock
¾-1 pint/425-570ml milk
Freshly ground black pepper
1½ oz/40g Danish Blue
cheese
Sea salt
Fresh celery leaves, sliced
chicory or croûtons, to garnish

Optional Advance Preparations

Up to 2 months ahead

1 Trim and thinly slice the celery. Peel and finely
chop the onion. Melt the butter in a large saucepan,
add the celery and onion and fry gently for about 10
minutes until the vegetables are soft but not coloured.
2 Stir in the stock (or water and stock cubes). Bring
to the boil, then reduce the heat and simmer covered
for about 20 minutes until the vegetables are soft
enough to mash. Purée in the blender. Cool and
freeze.

1 hour before serving

3 Put the block of frozen purée in a large saucepan
and set over gentle heat until thawed (alternatively
thaw in the microwave).

To assemble

4 Add the milk and bring to the boil. Season with
pepper.
5 Crumble in the cheese and remove from the heat.
Add salt only if necessary.
6 Serve hot with chunky wholemeal bread,
garnished with the celery leaves, sliced chicory or
croûtons.

Fresh Pears with Walnut Sauce

NC Serves **4**
Takes about 15 minutes

This is a light fruit starter to serve before a filling main course.

1 teaspoon clear honey
6 tablespoons mayonnaise (see
pages 29 or 37)
4 tablespoons thick natural
yogurt
2 William pears
2 oz/55g chopped walnuts
1 orange, sliced, for garnish

1 Stir the honey into the mayonnaise and mix in the yogurt.
2 Peel the pears, halve lengthwise and remove the core.
3 Put the pear halves cut side up in avocado dishes. Spoon the sauce on top and sprinkle with the walnuts.
4 Garnish the plates with halved orange slices.

Fried Banana Crisps

QC Serves **4-6**
Takes about 15 minutes

Ripe bananas are not suitable for deep frying. This recipe is also suitable as a curry accompaniment.

2 green bananas or *plantains*
Fresh sunflower oil for frying

1 Peel the bananas and slice them very thinly at a slight angle. Separate the slices on a plate or board.
2 One-third fill a deep pan with oil and heat until hazy. Slide the banana slices separately, but quickly, into the hot oil and fry until golden.
3 Remove from the pan with a slotted spoon and spread out on kitchen paper to drain. When the banana slices are cool sprinkle with salt and pepper.
4 Serve from a wooden bowl.

Gaspacho

Gaspacho ideally should be made with fresh tomatoes but tinned
tomatoes may be substituted.

2 lb/900g ripe tomatoes
2 green peppers
1 Spanish onion
1 large cucumber
1 garlic clove
2 tablespoons red wine vinegar
1 tablespoon sherry
Tabasco sauce
Celery salt
Finely ground black pepper

Optional Advance Preparations

Up to 48 hours ahead for refrigerator storage or up to
1 month ahead for freezer storage

1 Put the tomatoes in a saucepan and just cover with
water. Bring to the boil, then remove from the heat
and leave for 5 minutes. Press through a sieve into a
mixing bowl. Discard the skins and seeds.
2 Core, seed and finely dice the peppers. Finely chop
the onion and cucumber. Crush the garlic.
3 Add the vegetables to the tomato pulp. Stir in the
vinegar and sherry and add a shake of Tabasco.
4 Season with celery salt and some black pepper.
Chill for at least 2 hours.

To assemble

5 Serve with paprika croûtons (see page 31).

Grapefruit, Date and
Cashew Nut Indienne

Pink grapefruit are more expensive than the yellow sort but are
much sweeter and the flesh is a more delicate colour.

2 pink grapefruits
4 fresh dates
8-10 cashew nuts
2 oz/55g fromage blanc
2 pinches ground cardamom

1 Stand the grapefruits on a wooden board and
using a sharp knife peel vertically to reveal the flesh.
Cut out the segments over a bowl to catch the juices.
2 Slit the dates lengthwise, remove the stones and
slice into fine strips. Chop the nuts.
3 Arrange the grapefruit segments in a wheel fashion
around the sides of small flat plates and curve a strip
of date on top of each segment.
4 Mix the cheese and chopped nuts together. Place a
spoonful in the centre of the plates and dust with
cardamoms.

Grilled Grapefruit in Port

2 grapefruit
2 tablespoons port
1 teaspoon ground mixed spice
4 tablespoons raw cane granulated sugar

1   Halve the grapefruit and loosen the segments with a grapefruit knife. Pour the port over the cut surface and sprinkle with the spice and sugar.
2   Heat the grill. Put the grapefruit on a piece of foil in the grill pan and cook for about 5 minutes until hot and beginning to brown on the surface.
3   Serve on individual dishes.

Guacamole-stuffed Tomatoes

These can be prepared two or three hours in advance because the lime slice will prevent discoloration.

1 lime
4 large tomatoes
1 large avocado
Garlic salt
Tabasco
Freshly ground black pepper

1   Rinse and dry the lime. Using a zester, grate the rind from one half only. Cut a thick slice from one end of the lime and squeeze the juice into a medium bowl.
2   Stir in the grated zest. Slice the remaining lime for garnish.
3   Rinse and dry the tomatoes. Cut a thick slice from the round end and reserve. Using a teaspoon, scoop out all the pulp into a strainer over the bowl of lime juice, pressing with a wooden spoon.
4   Scrape the pulp underneath the strainer into the bowl. Discard the seeds.
5   Halve the avocado and, using the same teaspoon, scoop the flesh into the tomato and lime juices. Add a shake of garlic salt and a dash of Tabasco and plenty of pepper.
6   Mash the avocado with a potato masher or fork. Mix thoroughly to a smooth paste and spoon into the tomato shells. Cover with a slice of lime.
7   Cut a centre section from the tomato lids to form a handle and place on top.

Hummus

There are many recipes for hummus, a starter consisting of chick peas, sesame seed paste and lemon juice. This is a derivation of an old Lebanese recipe. It is usually served as a starter but can also be part of a main course, including dolmades, aubergine salad and green salad.

2×15 oz/432g tins chick peas
2 garlic cloves, peeled
5 tablespoons fresh lemon juice
1 teaspoon sea salt
½ teaspoon freshly ground black pepper
2 tablespoons water
6 tablespoons olive oil
5 tablespoons Tahini paste
Paprika

1 Drain the chick peas well and rinse to remove the sticky liquid. Set aside about 12 chick peas for garnish.
2 Put half the chick peas, the peeled garlic, all the lemon juice, salt, pepper and water in the blender and process until smooth. Add the remaining chick peas and the oil and process until smooth once more.
3 Add the Tahini paste, spoon by spoon. Process to a creamy purée. Taste and add extra lemon juice or water if the purée is too thick.
4 Spread the hummus thinly on individual plates, sprinkle with paprika and garnish with the reserved chick peas.
5 Serve with warmed wholemeal pitta bread and shredded lettuce.

Iced Cucumber Soup

When no ice-cubes are at hand chill the soup in the freezer for 15 minutes before serving.

2 firm cucumbers
6 ice cubes
½ teaspoon garlic salt
½ teaspoon white pepper
2 teaspoons dried tarragon
8 oz/225g low-fat Quark cheese

1 Peel the cucumber and reserve a 1 inch/2.5cm piece for garnish. Cut into small chunks and purée in the liquidizer with the ice-cubes, garlic salt, pepper, tarragon and Quark.
2 Pour into individual dishes and garnish with cucumber batons.

Leek and Lovage Salad _____ PA ★ Serves 4-5

Lovage has a flavour which is a cross between celery and parsley.
It was originally described as the love parsley.

3 slender young leeks
1 tablespoon sunflower oil
1 teaspoon fresh lemon juice
*1 teaspoon fresh chopped
lovage*
4-6 radishes
*6 tablespoons low-fat natural
yogurt*
¼ teaspoon sea salt
*¼ teaspoon freshly ground
black pepper*
Fresh lovage to garnish

Optional Advance Preparations

Up to 12 hours ahead

1 Use only the white part of the leeks. Wash
thoroughly, thinly slice and separate into rings.
2 Mix the oil and lemon juice with the lovage. Pour
over the leeks. Cover and refrigerate.
3 Wash the radishes and make four deep cuts around
the sides of each to form leaves. Soak the radishes in
ice-cold water in the refrigerator.

Half an hour before serving

4 Season the yogurt with salt and pepper and mix
with the marinated leeks.

To assemble

5 Drain the radishes, which should now resemble
flowers. Arrange the salad on individual plates and
top with a radish flower and fresh lovage.

Lemon Mint and Lime Water Ice _____PA Serves 4

Use a potato peeler to pare the rind from the limes. Invest in an ice-cream scoop and dip in cold water before each serving.

¾ pint/425ml water
4 oz/115g caster sugar
4 limes
2 handfuls fresh lemon mint
1 egg white and caster sugar, to decorate

Optional Advance Preparations

Up to 1 month ahead

1 Mix the water and sugar in a large saucepan. Thinly pare the rind from two limes and add to the saucepan. Bring to the boil and simmer for 5 minutes until lightly syrupy. Remove from the heat and stir in most of the mint. Cover and set aside for 10 minutes.
2 Squeeze the juice from the limes, reserve half and add the remainder to the syrup mixture. Strain into a shallow dish. (Freeze the reserved lime juice in ice cube trays to use in cool drinks.)
3 Open freeze until firm but not solid, then blend in the liquidizer. Pour back into the dish and freeze until firm, then cover and freeze until required.
4 Scrape out the four half shells and freeze separately.
5 Select a few small mint leaves and dip in egg white and sugar. Spread out on a plate covered with a disc of non-stick baking parchment and open freeze.

15 minutes before serving

6 Remove the water ice from the freezer.

To assemble

7 Fill the lime halves with a generous scoop of water ice and garnish with the crystallized mint leaves.

Melon, Ginger and Kiwi Petals

NC   Serves 5-6
Takes about 25 minutes

Take care when slicing the melon. It is probably safer to use a fork
and remember to position the knife blade away from your body.

1 honeydew melon
6–8 pieces stem ginger (from a
bottle of ginger in syrup)
2 kiwi fruit

1   Horizontally halve the melon. Scoop out the seeds
and drain the melon over a bowl to catch the juices.
Place the melon halves skin-side up on a board and
cut into eight wedges.
2   Using a stainless steel knife carve the flesh into
long thin slices. Arrange them petal fashion on
individual plates.
3   Slice the ginger, choosing the better shapes to
arrange on the melon petals towards the centre.
4   Slice, then peel the kiwis and place a middle cut
slice in the centre of the ginger.
5   Chop the reject ginger and kiwi pieces together
and put a spoonful on the kiwi slices. Refrigerate for
30 minutes.
6   Just before serving brush the melon with the
reserved juices.

Mushroom and Beansprout Soup

QC   Serves 6
Takes about 40 minutes

8 oz/225g onions
1½ oz/40g butter
12 oz/340g button mushrooms
1 oz/30g wholemeal flour
2 pints/1.1 litres hot vegetable
stock
½ teaspoon bayleaf powder
or 1 bay leaf
¼ teaspoon dried tarragon
Sea salt
Freshly ground black pepper
About 4 tablespoons sprouted
mung beans or beansprouts
2 tablespoons low-fat natural
yogurt

1   Finely chop the onions and using a large saucepan
sauté them in the butter until soft. Meanwhile rinse
and finely slice the mushrooms.
2   Add the flour to the pan of onions and cook for a
minute or two. Gradually add the stock, bay leaf
powder and tarragon and bring to the boil, stirring
occasionally.
3   Reserve about 8 mushroom slices and add the
remainder to the pan. Cover and simmer for 15
minutes. Season to taste with salt and pepper.
Remove bay leaf, if using.
4   Stir in the mung beans or beansprouts and bring
back to the boil. Remove from the heat and stir in
the yogurt.
5   Garnish with the reserved mushroom slices.

Orange Flowers

NC   Serves 4
Takes about 15 minutes

Although this is a no cook starter, there is no reason why it cannot
be prepared up to twelve hours ahead provided the oranges are kept
in a cool place.

4 soft-skinned oranges
About 4 oz/115g black grapes
Mint leaves to garnish

1 Using a sharp knife score through the orange peel
in seven equally spaced places from the stalk end to
within ¼ inch/5mm of the base.
2 Pull back the peel, then curl the ends inwards to
conceal the pith and tuck them firmly into the base.
3 Pull the orange segments apart but do not detach
them. With the sharp knife remove the membranes
from the segments.
4 Halve, de-seed, then roughly chop the grapes.
Spoon on to the oranges.
5 Garnish with mint leaves.

Pineapple and Walnut Pâté

NC   Serves 6
Takes about 10 minutes plus chilling

Only one slice of pineapple is used in this recipe. Unless you can
use the remainder of the pineapple it might be better to use frozen
or tinned pineapple in natural juice.

4 oz/115g cream cheese
6 tablespoons natural yogurt
½ teaspoon dill weed
1 slice pineapple
1 tablespoon walnut pieces
Freshly ground black pepper

1 Beat the cream cheese and yogurt together with
the dill weed.
2 Finely chop the pineapple and walnuts and mix
thoroughly into the cheese. Season sparingly with
pepper.
3 Spoon into a dish and chill for 30 minutes.
4 Garnish with fresh dill weed and serve with Melba
Toast (page 38).

Pumpkin Soup

PA   Serves 4-5

Pumpkins can weigh anything from 3 lb/1.35kg upwards. Large
pumpkins are cut up and sold by the pound. This is a low-fat recipe
which has the advantage of being plain rather than rich.

3 lb/1.35kg pumpkin
1 small onion
¾ pint/425ml vegetable stock
¾ pint/425ml milk
Sea salt
Freshly ground black pepper
Grated nutmeg
4 tablespoons low-fat natural yogurt
Chopped fried onions to garnish (see page 33)

Optional Advance Preparations

Up to 1 month ahead

1 Scoop out the seeds from the pumpkin and cut up the flesh. Finely chop the onion. Put into a large saucepan with the stock. Bring to the boil, then reduce the heat. Cover the pan with a lid and simmer for about 50 minutes or until tender.

2 Liquidize the soup, return to the pan and add the milk. Bring back to the boil, stirring all the time. Season with salt and pepper and nutmeg.

3 Leave to cool, then refrigerate or freeze.

To assemble

4 Thaw and reheat the soup in a saucepan or in the microwave. When thoroughly heated add extra milk if needed.

5 Stir in the yogurt and garnish with chopped fried onion.

Sesame Seed Fingers with Tahini Dip

QC ★ Serves 4-5
Takes about 20 minutes

The sesame fingers may be too hot to hold — add a fork to the place setting.

Dip

¼ pint/140ml mayonnaise
2 tablespoons tahini paste
1 teaspoon lemon juice
½ teaspoon garlic salt
¼ teaspoon freshly ground black pepper

2 eggs
¼ teaspoon sea salt
Some black pepper
6 slices wholemeal bread
4 tablespoons sesame seeds
Sunflower oil for frying

1 Put the mayonnaise in a jug or bowl and warm the base slightly in a bowl of very hot water. Remove from the heat.

2 Add the tahini paste, lemon juice, garlic salt and black pepper and beat until thick. Add 1 tablespoon milk to thin down if necessary.

3 Beat the eggs, salt and pepper in a jug. Remove the crusts from the bread and cut each slice into four fingers. Spread the sesame seeds on a plate or greaseproof paper.

4 Dip the bread fingers into the egg and then on to the sesame seeds. Pour about 1 inch/2.5cm oil into a large frying-pan. Heat well, then shallow fry the bread fingers a few at a time, turning them over as soon as the underside is brown (about 30 seconds).

Spring Cocktail

The lettuce in the bottom of the glasses will pack down if the cocktails are left for more than half an hour before serving. Keep back some shredded lettuce to top up the glasses if needed.

7 fl oz/200ml tomato juice
3 tablespoons mayonnaise (see pages 29 or 37)
1 teaspoon grated horseradish
Freshly ground black pepper
1 lettuce heart
1 large tomato
¼ cucumber
2 oz/55g Feta cheese
1 tablespoon sunflower seeds

1 Mix the tomato juice and mayonnaise with the horseradish and add some pepper. Chill while preparing the other ingredients.
2 Shred the lettuce. Peel and chop the tomatoes. Dice the cucumber and the cheese. Chop the sunflower seeds.
3 Put a little lettuce in each of four goblets. Mix the tomato, cucumber, cheese and seeds into the sauce. Spoon into the glasses.
4 Cover with the remaining shredded lettuce. Chill for 30 minutes.

Tomato Salad

Slightly green tomatoes taste much fresher than the all-over red kind. If you buy them ready packed the ripe are mixed with the unripe.

6 firm medium tomatoes
1 tablespoon fresh basil leaves
2 tablespoons medium red wine
Sea salt
Freshly ground black pepper
1 tablespoon walnut oil

1 Slice the tomatoes and put into a small wooden bowl. Sprinkle with the basil and spoon over the wine.
2 Season with salt and plenty of black pepper. Refrigerate for 1 hour to allow the flavours to mingle.
3 Just before serving sprinkle the oil over the surface.

Water Melon and Raspberry Soup

NC Serves 4-5
Takes about 30 minutes

A refreshing thin cold soup that could also be served as a dessert
after adding more honey.

1 small water melon
2 ice cubes
1 teaspoon clear honey
12 oz/340g raspberries, fresh
or thawed
½ pint/285ml rosé wine
¼ teaspoon ground allspice

1 Cut the melon into quarters. Remove as many
seeds as possible, then remove the flesh from the skin
with a sharp knife.

2 Cut up the water melon and purée in the blender
with the ice cubes, the honey and most of the
raspberries. Pour through a nylon strainer into a soup
tureen.

3 Stir in the wine. Add the allspice. Taste and add
more honey if you wish.

4 Garnish with the remaining raspberries.

Opposite *Canelloni Firenze (page 74).*

5 Main Courses

Although the main course is the centrepiece of a
meal, it does not have to be substantial. Follow a
filling starter with a lighter dish and choose the
dessert to follow accordingly.

I have endeavoured to make the book as flexible as
possible so that quite a number of main course dishes
are also suitable as starters. One main course recipe
would serve at least six as a starter. Those marked
with an asterisk are suitable choices.

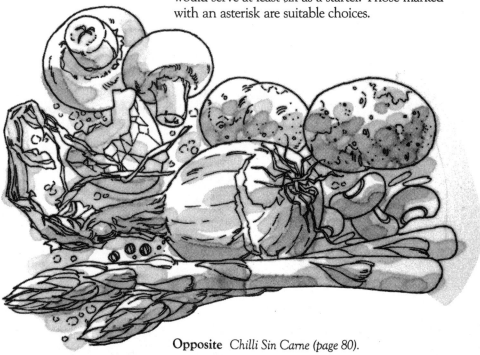

Opposite *Chilli Sin Carne (page 80).*

Almond Potato Croquettes
with Tomato Sauce_____PA Serves 4

The busy cook could be forgiven for using reconstituted dried
potatoes, but they are not in the same class.

1 ½ lb/680g large potatoes
6 tablespoons mayonnaise (see
pages 29 or 37)
Sea salt
Freshly ground black pepper
8 oz/225g whole almonds
2 eggs, beaten
½ pint/285ml tomato sauce
(see page 43)

Optional Advance Preparations

24 hours ahead

1 Peel, cut up and boil the potatoes in salted water
until soft. Drain and mash with mayonnaise and salt
and pepper to taste.
2 While the potatoes are cooking put the almonds in
a saucepan, cover with water and bring to the boil.
Drain and finely chop and put on to a plate.
3 With floured hands shape the potato into 8
croquettes, dip in the beaten egg and roll in the
chopped almonds, pressing the nuts well in. Chill in
the refrigerator.

To assemble

4 45 minutes before serving prepare a moderately hot
oven 375°F/190°C/Gas Mark 5.
5 Place the croquettes on a lightly oiled or lined
baking tray and bake until hot and crisp on the
outside. Meanwhile thaw and reheat the sauce.
6 Serve the croquettes with a green vegetable and
offer the sauce separately.

American Corn Fritters
with Broccoli Purée

QC ★ Serves 4
Takes about 35 minutes

Although best eaten hot, corn fritters can become quite addictive
and you may find yourself nibbling them when they are cold as
well.

1 lb/455g broccoli
Sea salt
½ teaspoon grated nutmeg
4 oz/115g wholemeal flour
1 teaspoon baking powder
¼ teaspoon paprika
¼ teaspoon sea salt
¼ teaspoon freshly ground
black pepper
2 eggs
¼ pint/140ml low-fat natural
yogurt
8 oz/225g cooked or tinned
sweetcorn
Sunflower oil for frying

1 Cut up the broccoli and cook in boiling salted
water until soft. Drain and purée with the nutmeg.
Return to the pan.
2 Mix the flour and baking powder, paprika, salt and
pepper in a bowl.
3 Separate the eggs and beat the whites until stiff.
Beat the egg yolks with 4 tablespoons of the yogurt.
4 Make a well in the centre of the flour, pour in the
blended yogurt and beat to a smooth batter.
5 Stir in the sweetcorn, then fold in the egg whites.
Pour about 2 inches/5cm of oil into a large saucepan.
Heat until one drop of the batter instantly sizzles,
then drop the batter into the oil, a teaspoon at a
time, making sure the fritters are well spaced out.
6 Flip the fritters over to ensure that both sides are
golden, and drain them on kitchen paper.
7 Keep the batches hot on a serving dish in a
moderate oven until all are cooked.
8 Reheat the broccoli purée in the saucepan or
microwave, then stir in the remaining yogurt and
season with salt and pepper.
9 Serve a pool of purée around individual servings of
fritters or in a separate bowl, placed in the centre of
the serving dish.

Asparagus and Cucumber Omelette ___QC ★ Serves 4
Takes about 30 minutes

Microwave owners can save about 10 minutes' cooking time by first
cooking the asparagus followed by the sauce.

1 bundle young asparagus
1 small cucumber
10 oz/285g tinned asparagus
tips
1 tablespoon sunflower oil
1 oz/30g plain white or
wholemeal flour
6 eggs
6 tablespoons yogurt
Sea salt
Freshly ground black pepper
About ¾ oz/20g butter

1 Break off the woody ends and scrape the stalks of
the fresh asparagus. Simmer in boiling water for 10
minutes or until just tender.
2 Halve the cucumber and cut one half into 2 inch/
5cm chunks, then cut into matchsticks.
3 Liquidize the tinned asparagus tips and their juice
with the remaining cucumber, roughly cut up. Add
the oil and flour. Pour into a saucepan and cook,
stirring all the time, until the sauce thickens. Cover
and keep warm.
4 Separate the eggs and beat the egg whites to soft
peaks. Beat the yolks and yogurt together and season
lightly. Fold in the egg whites.
5 Melt the butter in a large frying-pan, reducing the
quantity of butter if a non-stick pan is used. When
the butter is hot pour in the egg mixture. When the
underside is lightly brown lift one edge with a palette
knife and tilt the pan to allow the uncooked mixture
to flow underneath.
6 When the egg is just set on top, reverse it on to a
hot serving dish and arrange the freshly cooked
asparagus and raw cucumber sticks on top. Serve the
sauce separately.

Aubergine Soufflé _____PA   Serves 4

This soufflé contains no egg yolks, making it more suitable for
'heart watchers'.

1 large aubergine
Sea salt
1 oz/30g polyunsaturated
margarine
1 oz/30g plain white flour
1 teaspoon soya flour
1 tablespoon sunflower or soya
oil
¼ pint/140ml skimmed milk
Freshly ground black pepper
6 egg whites

Optional Advance Preparations

Up to 24 hours ahead

1 Halve the aubergines lengthwise and slash with a
sharp knife. Sprinkle with salt and leave for 30
minutes, then rinse in cold water. Remove the skin
and cut the flesh into chunks.
2 Heat the margarine and sauté the aubergines for
about 5 minutes. Stir, cover with a lid and cook over
the lowest possible heat for 30 minutes.
3 Blend the flour, soya flour, oil and milk in a
saucepan. Bring to the boil over low heat, stirring
continuously. Continue cooking until the sauce is as
thick as blancmange. Season with salt and pepper.
4 Liquidize or mash the aubergine with the sauce.
Cover and refrigerate.

To assemble

5 Up to 1 hour ahead prepare a moderately hot oven
375°F/195°C/Gas Mark 5. Grease a 7 inch/17cm
soufflé dish.
6 While the oven is heating up beat the egg whites
stiffly. Stir 1 tablespoon of the beaten whites into the
aubergine purée. Fold in the remainder with a
tablespoon.
7 Bake for 30-40 minutes — do not open the oven
for the first 20 minutes — until set on top. Serve
immediately.

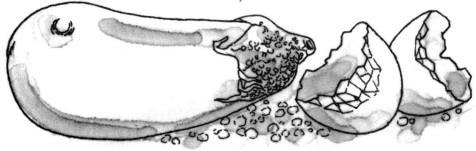

Baked Avocado

Don't buy avocados unless they are ripe. If the only ones available are slightly firm, they can be ripened in the airing cupboard in a polythene bag, best if nestling close to a banana, for about 24 hours. Those that are really hard take days to ripen and they are then often black inside.

1 thick slice wholemeal bread
2 tablespoons mayonnaise (see pages 29 or 37)
2 tablespoons soured cream
1 tablespoon fresh lemon juice
2 tablespoons chopped walnuts
1 tablespoon chopped chives
4 large avocados
1 tablespoon grated Parmesan cheese
Walnut-sized piece butter

1 Remove the crusts and mash the bread with the mayonnaise, soured cream and lemon juice. Mix in the walnuts and the chopped chives.
2 Cut the avocados into two sections, one being shallower than the other. Remove the stones.
3 Mash the flesh from the smaller sections with the walnut mixture. Pile on to the remaining avocados and sprinkle with the Parmesan, adding a dab of butter.
4 Bake in a fairly hot oven 400°F/200°C/Gas Mark 6 for 20 minutes or until the topping is brown.
5 Serve with freshly cooked bulgur cracked wheat.

Baked Spaghettini Puff

Spaghettini is a very thin type of spaghetti which cooks more quickly.

1 oz/30g butter
1 oz/30g wholemeal flour
¾ pint/425ml milk
3 oz/85g grated Cheddar cheese
½ teaspoon mustard powder
Freshly ground black pepper
4 oz/115g spaghettini
2 eggs

1 Preheat the oven to 400°F/200°C/Gas Mark 6.
2 Melt the butter in a saucepan and stir in the flour. Gradually add the milk and cook, beating continuously until the sauce thickens.
3 Cook for 1 more minute, then stir in the cheese, mustard and some black pepper.
4 Meanwhile cook the spaghettini in boiling salted water until tender, about 5 minutes.
5 Separate the eggs and beat the yolks into the sauce. Stir in the cooked spaghettini.
6 Stiffly beat, then fold in the egg whites.
7 Pour into a greased ovenproof dish and bake for about 25 minutes until lightly brown on top.
8 Serve with mange-tout and grilled tomatoes.

Bean and Cucumber Towers
with Cucumber Sauce

QC ★ Serves 4-6
Takes about 35 minutes

2 large cucumbers
6 oz/170g cooked borlotti
beans
2 tablespoons tomato purée
2 oz/55g grated Edam cheese
1 oz/30g cooked brown rice or
wholemeal breadcrumbs
Freshly ground black pepper
1 oz/30g butter
1 oz/30g wholemeal flour
1 oz/30g polyunsaturated
margarine
½ pint/285ml milk
Sea salt

1 Rinse the cucumber. Pare and set the skin aside. Cut the cucumber into 2 inch/5cm chunks. Remove the centres with an apple corer and set aside.
2 Mash the beans with the tomato purée and mix in the cheese with the rice or breadcrumbs. Season with plenty of pepper.
3 Place the cucumber chunks in a lightly greased casserole dish. Fill the cucumber cavities with bean mixture. Top with dabs of butter.
4 Cover with the lid and cook in a fairly hot oven 400°F/200°C/Gas Mark 6 for about 20 minutes until hot.
5 Meanwhile prepare the sauce. Sieve the flour into a saucepan, reserving the bran. Add the margarine and milk. Cook over a moderate heat, stirring continuously until the sauce thickens.
6 Stir in the bran, cucumber peel and the reserved centres. Cook for a further 2 minutes. Liquidize the sauce and season with salt and pepper.
7 Reheat the sauce and serve with the baked cucumber.

Bower Pie

This is an economical dish to cook when tomatoes are plentiful.

1 lb/455g ripe tomatoes
2 medium onions
3 oz/85g Leicester cheese
6 oz /170g wholemeal
breadcrumbs
1 oz/30g desiccated coconut
2 tablespoons freshly chopped
basil
Salad oil
Sea salt
Freshly ground black pepper
1 tablespoon dry red wine
1 oz/30g rye flakes
1 oz/30g butter

Optional Advance Preparations

Up to 6 hours ahead

1 Slice the tomatoes. Peel and finely slice the onions. Grate the cheese and mix with the breadcrumbs, coconut and basil.
2 Lightly oil an 8 inch/20cm pie dish. Spread half the cheese, crumbs and basil in the bottom and add layers of tomatoes and onion slices.
3 Sprinkle each layer with salt and pepper and a few drops of wine. Spread the remaining crumbs and the rye flakes over and top with dabs of butter. Refrigerate.

To assemble

4 About 1 hour ahead heat the oven to 375°F/190°C/Gas Mark 5. Put the pie in the centre of the oven and bake for 50 minutes or until golden.
5 Serve hot with steamed courgettes and crisp cooked spring cabbage.

Brussels Sprouts Amandine with Hot Tabbouleh

_____PA   Serves 4

Avoid using frozen sprouts in this recipe as they do not cook up as
well as freshly picked sprouts early in the season.

Tabbouleh

*4 oz/115g bulgur cracked
wheat*
*¾ pint/425ml plus 2
tablespoons hot water*
Small handful parsley sprigs
2 tablespoons safflower oil
2 tablespoons fresh lemon juice
Sea salt
Freshly ground black pepper

Brussels Sprouts Amandine

1 small onion
1 oz/30g butter
2 oz/55g flaked almonds
1 teaspoon tarragon leaves
Sea salt
Freshly ground black pepper
*About 1 lb/455g Brussels
sprouts*

Optional Advance Preparations

Up to one month ahead

1 Part prepare the Tabbouleh. Put the bulgur cracked
wheat and water in a large saucepan, bring to the
boil, then reduce the heat. Put a tight-fitting lid on
the pan and cook gently for about 5 minutes.
2 Add 2 tablespoons hot water. Replace the lid,
remove from the heat and leave to cool. Freeze in a
tightly sealed container or refrigerate for up to two
days.

Up to one week ahead

3 Prepare the Amandine. Finely chop the onion and
sauté in the butter for about a minute. Add the
almond flakes and sauté until they are brown. Add
the tarragon and salt and pepper to taste.
4 Leave to cool, then freeze in a well-sealed container
or store in the refrigerator for up to 24 hours.

To assemble

5 Thaw the Tabbouleh and reheat gently in a
colander over a pan of simmering water for about 10
minutes or in the microwave for 3-4 minutes on full
power.
6 Chop and add the parsley, oil, lemon juice and salt
and pepper to taste. Keep hot.
7 Turn out the Amandine mixture into a large
saucepan and put over low heat to melt.
8 Trim, wash and halve the sprouts and add to the
pan. Put on the lid and cook gently, shaking the pan
frequently until the sprouts are tender, about 10
minutes.
9 Arrange the Tabbouleh on a hot serving dish and
pile the sprouts and almond mixture on top. Garnish
with a few sprigs of fresh tarragon.

Cannelloni Firenze

Use fresh pasta squares or ready-to-bake cannelloni tubes.

*12 oz/340g carton frozen
chopped spinach
4 oz/115g curd cheese
4 oz/115g cottage cheese
¼ teaspoon grated nutmeg
2 tablespoons grated Parmesan
2 eggs
Freshly ground black pepper
12-15 ready-to-bake
cannelloni tubes*

Sauce

*2 oz/55g butter
1 oz/30g flour
½ teaspoon sea salt
¼ teaspoon cayenne
¼ teaspoon bay leaf powder
¾ pint/425ml milk*

Topping

*2-3 tea rusks
2 tablespoons grated Parmesan
About ½ oz/15g butter*

1 Preheat the oven to 425°F/220°C/Gas Mark 7.
2 Thaw and drain the spinach. Beat with the curd cheese, cottage cheese, nutmeg, Parmesan and eggs and add some black pepper.
3 Fill the cannelloni tubes with the mixture and arrange seam-side down in a well-greased baking dish.
4 Put all the sauce ingredients in a saucepan. Cook over moderate heat, stirring continuously, until the sauce thickens. Continue cooking for another minute.
5 Pour the sauce over the cannelloni. Crush the rusks and sprinkle over the sauce. Top with dabs of butter and the cheese.
6 Bake for 20-25 minutes until bubbling and browned on top.
7 Serve with a salad of Chinese leaves and sliced onion rings.

Casserole Fazolia

Tinned cannellini or butter beans are perfectly acceptable
substitutes for the haricot beans and they are so easy to obtain in
tins. Buy an extra tin just in case the actual weight of beans is low.

1 large onion
2 celery sticks
8 oz/225g smoked tofu
3-4 tablespoons sunflower oil
8 oz/225g tin tomatoes
1 tablespoon tomato purée
Freshly ground black pepper
Sea salt
1 lb/455g cooked haricot
beans
Black olives
Pearl onions

1 Chop the onion and the celery.
2 Drain the tofu and pat dry with kitchen paper.
Cut into cubes.
3 Heat the oil in a saucepan. Fry the cubed tofu
until firm. Remove from the pan and drain on
kitchen paper.
4 Fry the onion and celery until brown. Empty the
tin of tomatoes into the pan, add the tomato purée
and season with plenty of black pepper.
5 Reduce the heat and simmer for about 10 minutes
until thickened. Fold in the beans and tofu, taking
care not to mash the tofu, and heat for 5 minutes.
Add salt to taste.
6 Pour on to a heated serving dish and garnish with
black olives and tiny bottled pearl onions.

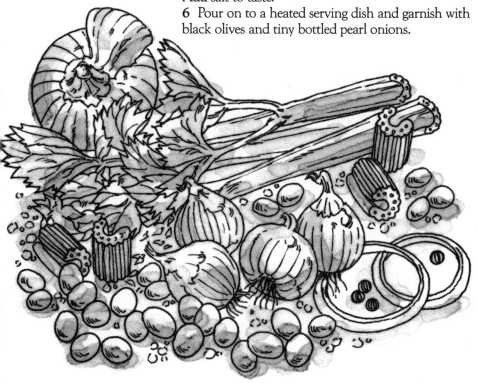

Cauliflower Niçoise

QC Serves 4
Takes about 25 minutes

Some supermarkets sell packs of fresh cauliflower florets. After cooking reshape them by packing them floret-side down into a 1 pint/0.55 litre pudding basin, reverse them on to a heated serving dish, then add the nuts and sauce.

1 large cauliflower
1 medium onion
4 medium tomatoes
4 black olives
1 oz/30g butter
1 garlic clove
1 teaspoon dried oregano
Sea salt
Freshly ground black pepper
2 oz/55g flaked almonds

1 Trim and cook the cauliflower in plenty of boiling salted water until the florets are tender. Drain and carefully remove the florets. Retain the outside.
2 Meanwhile peel and slice the onion. Chop the tomatoes. Chop and stone the olives.
3 Melt the butter and fry the garlic and onion. Add the tomatoes, olives and oregano and fry until the vegetables are hot. Season with salt and pepper.
4 Rebuild the cauliflower florets into the cauliflower casing, inserting the nuts between the florets. Pour the sauce over the top.
5 Serve with boiled new potatoes and green beans.

Chequerboard Grill with Port and Carrot Purée

PA   Serves 4-5

Two kinds of nut patties served in an unusual way with a carrot
and tomato purée.

Hazelnut and cashew chequers

4 oz/115g toasted hazelnuts
4 oz/115g cashew nuts
4 oz/115g wholemeal bread
1 celery stick
2 oz/55g mushrooms
1 small onion
1 oz/30g butter
¾ oz/20g wholemeal flour
¼ pint/140ml milk
2 tablespoons tomato purée
2 eggs
1 tablespoon soya sauce
Sea salt
Freshly ground black pepper

Purée

12 oz/340g carrots
¼ teaspoon caraway seeds
2 medium tomatoes
1 tablespoon port
Sea salt
Freshly ground black pepper

Optional Advance Preparations

Up to 24 hours ahead

1 Very finely chop the nuts. Finely chop the bread.
Separately chop the celery, mushrooms and onion.
2 Melt the butter in a saucepan, stir in the onion
and sauté for 3 minutes. Stir in the flour, cook for
about 1 minute, then gradually add the milk. Cook,
stirring all the time, until the mixture is thick.
3 Put half the sauce into a bowl. Into this mixture
add the hazelnuts, half the breadcrumbs, celery,
tomato purée, 1 egg and salt and pepper to taste.
4 Using the remaining sauce stir in the cashew nuts,
remaining breadcrumbs, soya sauce, mushrooms, 1
egg and salt and pepper to taste.
5 Shape each mixture into a square about ½ inch/
1cm thick, working on a floured surface. Leave to
cool, then place on greased foil, wrap and refrigerate.

Make the purée

6 Scrape the carrots, cut into chunks and boil in
lightly-salted water, adding the caraway seeds. Drain
and purée with the quartered tomatoes, port, salt and
pepper to taste. Cool, cover and refrigerate.

To assemble

7 Half an hour before serving, cut each nut mixture
into sixteen squares. Place the squares on a large
greased baking tray and bake in a hot oven
400°F/200°C/Gas Mark 6 for 15 minutes.
8 Reheat purée on hob or in a covered casserole in
the oven.
9 Serve two or three of each kind to each guest,
pouring a pool of purée around.

Cheese and Lentil Pie _____ PA Serves 4-5

Take a little extra time to decorate the top of the pie and then this
simple dish will be a much admired centrepiece. If you cannot spare
the pie dish for a stay in the freezer, first line it with foil and when
the recipe is frozen, it will be a simple matter to lift it out of the dish.

Pastry

5 oz/140g vegetable suet
8 oz/225g wholemeal plain
flour
1 egg
3 tablespoons cold water
2 tablespoons milk
¼ teaspoon sea salt

Filling

6 oz/170g red lentils
1 medium onion
½ oz/15g butter
4 oz/115g strong grated cheese
1 tablespoon freshly chopped
parsley
1 egg
Sea salt
Freshly ground black pepper

Optional Advance Preparations

Up to 1 month ahead

1 Put the suet in the freezer until hard. Rinse the
lentils and put in a saucepan with plenty of water.
Bring to the boil, then simmer for 15-20 minutes
until soft. Drain.

2 Finely chop the onion and fry in the butter until
soft. Stir in the lentils, cheese and parsley. Beat in the
egg and season to taste with salt and pepper. Leave to
cool.

3 Make the pastry. Put the flour into a bowl. Grate
in the vegetable suet. Beat the egg with the water,
milk and salt and sprinkle over the pastry mixture.
Stir with a fork to a soft dough. Add extra water if
necessary.

4 Gather into a ball with floured hands. Divide into
two and press one into the base and sides of a 8 inch/
20cm round lightly greased pie dish and set aside the
other until you have filled the base with the lentil
mixture.

5 Roll out the remaining piece on plenty of flour to a
circle just bigger than the dish. Fit on to the dish,
moistening the edges so that they seal. Flute or pinch
the edges decoratively and use pastry trimmings to
make leaves. Brush with beaten egg.

6 Open freeze until the pastry is firm, then overwrap
and store in the freezer.

Two hours ahead

7 Transfer the pie to the refrigerator to start the
thawing process.

One hour ahead

8 Heat the oven to 400°F/200°C/Gas Mark 6.
When the oven is hot put the pie dish on to a baking
tray and bake for 30 minutes. Reduce the heat to
350°F/180°C/Gas Mark 4 for about 40 minutes to
enable the filling to cook properly.

To assemble

9 Serve hot with plain cooked carrots and spring
greens.

Chicory Walnut Salad

NC ★ Serves 4
Takes about 30 minutes

A dainty dish for small appetites. Choose pale chicory with yellow
but not green-tinged edges.

2 tablespoons walnut oil
1 tablespoon cider vinegar
¼ pint/140ml low-fat natural
yogurt
Pinch dark brown sugar
Sea salt
Freshly ground black pepper
8 small heads chicory
2 oz/55g refreshed walnuts
(see page 23)
2 red dessert apples
4 oz/115g carton cottage
cheese

1 Beat the oil, vinegar and yogurt together and
season with the sugar, salt and pepper.
2 Trim the chicory and separate the leaves from four
of the heads and finely slice the remainder. Chop the
walnuts.
3 Peel, core and slice the apples and mix into the
dressing with the walnuts and sliced chicory.
4 Arrange the chicory leaves in petal fashion on a
serving dish and pile the apple mixture into the
centre.
5 Using a potato baller scoop tiny balls of cottage
cheese from the carton and arrange round the apple
mixture.

Chilli Sin Carne _____PA Serves 4

Folded flour tortillas briefly warmed in the oven will go well with this dish and a crisp green salad will be welcomed by your guests.

Chilli

8 oz/225g kidney beans
1 teaspoon fennel seeds
1 large onion
1 clove garlic
1 tablespoon sunflower oil
1-2 teaspoons chilli compound powder
1 teaspoon ground cumin
1×14 oz/400g tin chopped tomatoes
1×8 oz/227g tin pimientos
¼ pint/140ml red wine
Sea salt
Freshly ground black pepper
½ teaspoon bay leaf powder

Sauce

2 avocados
1 garlic clove
2 tablespoons sunflower oil
1 teaspoon Herbes de Provence
2 tablespoons fresh lemon juice
Sea salt
Freshly ground black pepper

Optional Advance Preparations

Up to 4 days ahead

1 Soak the kidney beans overnight in cold water. Drain, rinse and put in a large saucepan with about 2 pints/1.1 litres cold water. Bring to the boil and cook in fast bubbling water for 10 minutes. Add the fennel seeds. Reduce the heat and simmer covered for 45 minutes or until soft. Top up with extra boiling water during cooking if needed. Drain.
2 Finely chop the onion and garlic and fry in a large saucepan in the oil until the onion begins to brown.
3 Stir in the chilli compound powder, ground cumin, the chopped tomatoes, well drained pimientos and the wine. Bring to the boil and without covering simmer until fairly thick.
4 Season with salt and pepper and add the bay leaf powder. Stir in the cooked kidney beans. Leave to cool, then cover and refrigerate or freeze.

Up to 2 hours ahead

5 Remove the chilli mixture from the freezer. Place in a saucepan or covered casserole. Thaw over the lowest possible heat on the hob or in the oven at 350°F/180°C/Gas Mark 4. Stir occasionally after thawing.

To assemble

6 Make the sauce. Peel and cut up the avocado flesh. Purée in the blender with the garlic, oil and herbs and 1 tablespoon lemon juice. Season with salt and pepper.
7 Pour into a jug and sprinkle with the remaining lemon juice. Cover and set aside until ready to serve. Pour the sauce over the chilli just before serving.

Colcannon with Kidney Bean Sauce

QC   Serves 4-5
___Takes about 35 minutes

Even plain dishes when well cooked and well presented can be
served at the best of dinner parties. For vegans use water instead of
the milk.

1 lb/455g large potatoes
Sea salt
1 lb/455g cabbage
2 bunches large spring onions
1 oz/30g margarine
1×15 oz/432g tin red kidney
beans
5 tablespoons milk
1 teaspoon arrowroot
Freshly ground black pepper
1 tablespoon rosemary leaves
1 teaspoon fresh lemon juice

1 Peel the potatoes and slice thinly. Cook in boiling
water for about 5 minutes until tender. Meanwhile
wash the cabbage and slice thinly.
2 Finely slice the spring onions. Remove the potatoes
with a slotted spoon. Put the cabbage into the potato
water, add a teaspoon of margarine. Cover and cook
for about 10 minutes.
3 While the cabbage is cooking drain the beans and
put in the blender with the milk and arrowroot but
do not process. Remove the cabbage from the
cooking liquid but do not throw the liquid away.
4 Put a layer of cabbage in a greased shallow flameproof dish. Sprinkle with salt, pepper and rosemary.
5 Cover with a layer of spring onions and potatoes
and spread thinly with margarine. Repeat the layers,
finishing with potato. Put the dish under a medium
grill to brown.
6 Add sufficient cooking liquid to the blender to
make up to 1 pint/570ml. Add the fresh lemon juice
and process until smooth, then return to the
saucepan and bring to the boil, stirring continuously
until the sauce thickens. Season with salt and pepper.
7 Serve the sauce separately with each portion.

Courgette, Celery and Borlotti Salad

QC ★ Serves 4
Takes about 15 minutes

Tinned borlotti beans should be well rinsed before using.

2 medium courgettes
1 small onion
1 small green pepper
3 celery sticks
Garlic salt
6 tablespoons cooked borlotti beans
2 tablespoons safflower oil
1 tablespoon cider vinegar
1 tablespoon tomato ketchup
Freshly ground black pepper

1 Top and tail the courgettes and cut into quarters lengthwise, then into ½ inch/1cm slices.
2 Peel and finely chop the onion. Seed, core and dice the green pepper. Finely slice the celery.
3 Put all these vegetables in a saucepan, just cover with water and add a generous shake of garlic salt. Put the lid on the pan and cook for 5 minutes or until just tender, shaking the pan occasionally.
4 Pour into a colander and cool under cold running water. Drain thoroughly. Mix in the borlotti beans and turn into a salad bowl.
5 Beat the oil, vinegar and tomato ketchup and some black pepper together. Pour evenly over the salad.
6 Serve with sautéed potatoes.

Crofters Salad

Serve hot or warm. Scrambled eggs can become leathery when cold.

1 small onion
1-1½ lb/455-680g small new potatoes
Sea salt
1×15 oz/425g tin flageolet beans
8 oz/225g fresh or frozen French beans
6 oz/170g fresh or frozen peas
8-9 tablespoons low-calorie mayonnaise
1 tablespoon freshly chopped parsley
1 tablespoon chopped chives
Freshly ground black pepper
4 eggs
4 tablespoons milk or water

1 Peel and finely slice the onion into rings. Scrub and boil the potatoes in salted water. Drain the flageolet beans.

2 Cook the French beans and peas together, adding the flageolet beans towards the end of cooking. Drain thoroughly.

3 Mix together the mayonnaise, parsley, chives and some black pepper, then stir into the drained vegetables.

4 Beat the eggs with 4 tablespoons cold milk or water and season with salt and pepper.

5 Soft scramble the eggs in a non-stick pan or in the microwave. Spread over the hot salad and garnish with the onion rings.

6 Serve the potatoes separately.

Crudités _____NC ★ Serves 5-6

Crudités are a classic French way of serving raw vegetables.
They make a refreshing meal to eat at any season.

Dressing
1 lemon
8 tablespoons sunflower oil
½ teaspoon soft brown sugar
½ teaspoon sea salt
⅓ teaspoon mustard powder
*½ teaspoon freshly ground
black pepper*

Vegetables
1 medium red pepper
1 medium green pepper
4 medium tomatoes
1 large firm courgette
8 oz/225g carrots
6 oz/170g cauliflower florets
1 very small celeriac
2 teaspoons capers
*8 tablespoons mayonnaise
(see pages 29 or 37)*

1 Cut the lemon in half lengthwise and squeeze the juice into a large bowl. Scrape out and reserve the empty shells.

2 Add the remaining dressing ingredients and beat well.

3 Prepare the vegetables. Core, de-seed and thinly slice the peppers into rings. Cut each tomato into eight sections. Cut the courgette into matchstick-sized strips. Scrape and coarsely grate the carrots. Cut the cauliflower into bite-sized florets.

4 Put the dressing in a bowl. Peel and coarsely grate the celeriac into the bowl and stir thoroughly.

5 Arrange the peppers alternately around the edges of a serving dish and on the inside place a circle of the tomato sections.

6 Remove the celeriac with a slotted spoon from the bowl, allowing it to drain well and arrange in a wedge-shaped section on the dish.

7 Next immerse the carrot in the dressing. Remove it, allowing the marinade to drain back into the bowl. Place in a wedge shape opposite the celeriac.

8 Now repeat with the courgette and then with the cauliflower. There should now be four 'V' shaped sections of different vegetables almost filling the centre of the dish.

9 Chop the capers and mix with the mayonnaise. Spoon into the empty lemon shells and place one in the middle of the dish and reserve the other to replenish as necessary.

10 Serve with separate bowls of mixed nuts, raisins and home-baked crisps (see page 36).

Danish Cucumber

I have used lightly-cooked firm courgettes in place of cucumber at
times and in fact raw courgettes also are delicious.

1 large cucumber
2 hard-boiled eggs
2 tablespoons roasted peanuts
2 small red peppers
2 tablespoons cooked chick
peas
Sea salt
Freshly ground black pepper
Paprika

1 Top and tail the cucumber and cut across into four
sections. Cut each section in half lengthwise. Scoop
out the seeds.
2 Finely chop the eggs. Chop the peanuts. Core,
seed and cut the peppers into rings.
3 Mix the eggs, peanuts and chick peas with the
cucumber seeds and season with salt and pepper. Pile
on to the cucumber and add a sprinkle of paprika.
4 Arrange the pepper rings around the edge of a
serving dish and place the cucumber pyramids on
top.

Devilish Mushrooms

Most of the ingredients for this recipe are store-cupboard items.
Chick peas can be obtained in tins and double cream may be long
life or frozen.

*4 or 5×1 inch/2.5cm thick
slices bread cut from a large
granary loaf
Vegetable oil
½ clove garlic
1 lb/455g tiny button
mushrooms
Juice of ½ lemon
5 tablespoons cooked chick
peas
5 tablespoons double creamed
1 tablespoon tomato purée
1 tablespoon creamed
horseradish
1 tablespoon Holbrook's sauce
2 teaspoons French mustard
Few drops Tabasco
Freshly ground black pepper
Parsley sprigs to garnish*

1 Cut out large rounds from the bread using an
upturned basin or pastry cutter. Press a small cutter
on to each to reach nearly to the bottom. Carefully
remove the loosened piece to form a lid.
2 Rub a large frying-pan with the cut garlic. Add a
few tablespoons of oil to the pan and heat, then
shallow fry the bread cases and lids on both sides
until crisp and golden. It may be necessary to add
extra oil in between each batch. Remove the fried
bread and drain on kitchen paper.
3 Drain most of the oil from the pan, then add the
mushrooms and sauté for about 2 minutes. Stir in the
lemon juice and chick peas and cook until hot.
4 Put the bread cases on an ovenproof serving platter
and spoon the mushrooms into the centre.
5 Cut the lids in half and reheat on a separate
baking tray. Place in a moderate oven for 5 minutes to
ensure that the mushrooms are piping hot.
6 Meanwhile stir the cream, tomato purée,
horseradish, Holbrook's sauce, mustard, Tabasco and
some black pepper into the juices left in the pan.
Heat, stirring all the time, but do not boil.
7 To serve, pour the sauce over the mushrooms,
arrange two lid halves butterfly fashion on top and
garnish with the parsley.

Dolmades

Unless you live in the country of origin, you will have to buy vine
leaves in tins or vacuum packs. There may seem to be a large
number of ingredients in this recipe but they are all stock items or
easy to obtain.

6 oz/170g brown rice
Juice of 2 lemons
20-30 vine leaves (available in tins)
2 shallots
2 teaspoons chopped mint
1 tablespoon dried parsley
2 eggs
Sea salt
Freshly ground black pepper
1 oz/30g pine nuts
8 oz/227g tin tomatoes
1 tablespoon olive oil
About 1 pint/570ml hot stock
1 oz/30g butter
½ oz/15g wholemeal flour

Optional Advance Preparations

24 hours ahead

1 Part cook the rice in plenty of boiling salted water until the outside of the grains are soft but inside they are still raw. Drain and mix with the juice of 1 lemon.

2 Meanwhile drain the vine leaves. Heat a saucepan of water until boiling. Plunge the vine leaves in the water and bring back to the boil. Dip each leaf in cold water. Drain and set aside.

3 Put the shallots, mint, parsley and one egg in a bowl and season with salt and pepper. Mix with the rice and chopped pine nuts.

4 Put a teaspoon of the rice filling on one edge of each vine leaf. Roll the leaf over once, tuck in both sides and continue rolling up.

5 Empty the tin of tomatoes into a deep frying- or sauté pan and mash with a fork. Tightly pack with a layer of dolmades seam-side down. Should your pan be too small add a second layer of dolmades, separated with flat vine leaves. Sprinkle with the oil.

6 Put a small plate on top of the dolmades to keep them flat. Pour in the stock until it reaches 1 inch/2.5cm above the plate. Bring to the boil, then reduce the heat and poach for 30-40 minutes, shaking the pan occasionally to prevent sticking. Top up the liquid if necessary.

7 Cover and leave to cool in the refrigerator.

30 minutes ahead

8 Reheat the dolmades in the pan. Remove them with a slotted spoon, cover tightly and keep warm.

To assemble

9 Beat the second egg and mix with the juice of the remaining lemon. Melt the butter in a small saucepan and stir in the flour. Add ½ pint/285ml of the dolmades liquid or stock.

10 Cook, stirring vigorously, until the sauce thickens. Remove from the heat and stir in the egg and lemon juice. Season with salt and pepper. Pour over the warm dolmades and serve two, three or four to each person. An olive salad and Feta cheese make a pleasant accompaniment.

Enchiladas Sante Fé

QC   Serves 4-6
Cooking time about 45 minutes

You can make your own tortillas in advance if you wish.
You will find the recipe for these among the basic recipes.

1 oz/30g butter
1 small shallot, finely chopped
4 red chillis (available in
bottles), chopped
14 oz/400g tin chopped
tomatoes
1 teaspoon mixed dried herbs
½ teaspoon celery salt
Freshly ground black pepper
2 eggs
¼ pint/140ml natural yogurt
½ pint/285ml single cream
4 tortillas or 2 wholemeal
pitta bread
6 oz/170g grated Edam cheese
Small packet tortilla chips

1 Melt the butter in a saucepan and sauté the shallot for about 2 minutes.
2 Halve, de-seed and chop the chillis. Add to the pan with the tomatoes, herbs, celery salt and some black pepper. Simmer for 5 minutes, then remove from the heat.
3 Beat the eggs with half the yogurt and half the cream, and then stir into the tomato mixture — this may curdle a little but does not affect the finished dish. Beat the remaining yogurt and cream and set aside.
4 Tear the tortillas or pittas in pieces and put a layer in the bottom of an ovenproof dish. Cover with a layer of sauce and grated cheese.
5 Repeat the layers, finishing with tortillas or pitta. Pour the reserved yogurt mixture over the top and sprinkle with tortilla chips.
6 Bake in a moderate oven 350°F/180°C/Gas Mark 4 for 20-30 minutes.
7 Serve hot with a green salad.

Falafel

Falafel is a Middle Eastern snack that is high in protein.
In this recipe bulgur cracked wheat is added for extra nutrition.

8 oz/225g chick peas
2 tablespoons bulgur cracked wheat
2 slices wholemeal bread
2 garlic cloves
2 tablespoons freshly chopped parsley
1 teaspoon sea salt
¼ teaspoon paprika
½ teaspoon ground cumin
½ teaspoon coriander
¼ teaspoon freshly ground black pepper
Wholemeal flour for coating
Sunflower oil for frying

Optional Advance Preparations

Up to 36 hours ahead

1 Soak the chick peas overnight in cold water. Drain. Put the chick peas in a saucepan with about 2 pints/ 1.1 litres cold water. Bring to the boil, then simmer for 2 hours until very soft, topping up with hot water if necessary. Drain and mash to a smooth paste.

Up to 24 hours ahead

2 Put the bulgur cracked wheat in a bowl and cover with hot water. Leave for 20 minutes, then drain.
3 Meanwhile dip the bread in cold water and squeeze out with your hands. Mash into the chick pea paste. Crush and add the garlic, parsley, salt, paprika, cumin, coriander and pepper.
4 Add the drained bulgur and mix thoroughly. Cover and refrigerate or freeze.

About 1 hour before serving

5 Divide the mixture into 1 inch/2.5cm balls and lightly dust with flour.

About 30 minutes before serving

6 Cook the Falafel. Heat about 2 inches/5cm fresh oil in a deep pan and fry a few at a time, making sure that all the sides are golden brown. Drain on kitchen paper.

To assemble

7 Serve hot in pitta bread with a green salad or with ratatouille.

Falcon Hotel Fondue

QC ★ Serves 4-5
Takes about 20 minutes

I was delighted to be offered an 'interesting' vegetarian dish in this
sixteenth-century inn in Bridgnorth.

2 small courgettes
2×1 inch/2.5cm thick slices
wholemeal bread
8 oz/225g grated Gruyère
cheese
2 tablespoons cornflour
¼ pint/140ml milk
Freshly ground black pepper
½ pint/285ml dry white wine
1 teaspoon Kirsch
8 oz/225g button mushrooms

1 Rinse, top and tail the courgettes and cut into
½ inch/1cm slices. Cut the bread into cubes and toast
in the grill pan, turning to brown them on all sides.
Pile into a wooden bowl.
2 Mix the cheese and cornflour in a heavy-based
saucepan. Add the milk and season with plenty of
black pepper. Heat gently, stirring continuously, until
the cheese has melted.
3 Stir in the wine and Kirsch and cook over low
heat, stirring continuously until bubbling.
4 Add the mushrooms and courgettes. Simmer for
5-7 minutes.
5 Pour into hot individual pie dishes and serve at
once with the toast cubes.

Ginger Tofu Chow Mein

QC   Serves 4
Takes about 25 minutes

1 small onion
4 oz/115g beansprouts
8 oz/225g tin water chestnuts
1×10 oz/280g bamboo shoots
4 tablespoons mayonnaise (see pages 29 or 37)
1 tablespoon shoyu
1 teaspoon freshly grated ginger root
Freshly ground black pepper
5 oz/150g Chinese noodles
Vegetable oil for frying
8 oz/225g tofu

1 Chop the onion, rinse and drain the beansprouts, drain the water chestnuts and drain the bamboo shoots.
2 Mix the mayonnaise, shoyu and ginger root with some black pepper. Combine in a salad bowl with the vegetables.
3 Cook the noodles in boiling water according to the directions on the packet. Drain thoroughly.
4 Deep fry in vegetable oil, tossing until crispy. Drain on kitchen paper.
5 Pat the tofu dry, then cube and fry lightly in the oil. Drain well. Arrange the tofu on the salad and top with fried noodles. Serve at once.

Green Meadow Basket _____PA Serves 4

A basket of deep-fried potato shreds filled with broccoli and
sunflower seeds in a cheese-flavoured sauce.

1 lb/455g large potatoes
Oil for frying
3-4 spring onions
1½ oz/45g butter
1 tablespoon sunflower seeds
½ teaspoon mustard powder
Pinch dried oregano
1 oz/30g wholemeal flour
1 pint/570ml milk
*1 vegetable stock cube,
crumbled*
About 1 lb/455g broccoli
*About 4 oz/115g Cheddar
cheese, grated*

Optional Advance Preparations

Up to 2 days ahead

1 Prepare the potatoes. Peel, rinse and finely shred or
coarsely grate, using a food processor. Rinse in several
changes of cold water to remove the starch, then pat
dry in a clean tea towel. Using paper towels is not a
good idea as I have got through half a roll without
completing the job.

2 Have ready a dish lined with kitchen paper, and a
slotted spoon. Pour about 1½ inches/4cm vegetable
oil into a saucepan. Put the pan over moderate heat
and when the oil is very hot (375°F/190°C), add the
potato shreds a handful at a time and stir with a fork.
As soon as the shreds rise to the surface and are
golden remove with the slotted spoon and drain on
to the prepared dish. Continue frying until all the
potato is cooked.

3 Remove the pan from the heat and cover with the
lid to keep out dust until you have time to strain the
oil. Leave the fried potatoes until cool, then store in
an airtight container.

Up to 24 hours ahead

4 Trim and finely slice the spring onions and sauté in
the butter for a minute or two. Add the sunflower
seeds and cook for another minute.

5 Stir in the mustard powder, oregano and flour.
Remove the pan from the heat and blend in the milk.
Add the stock cube.

6 Return the pan to the heat and cook, stirring
continuously until the sauce thickens. Leave to cool,
then cover the surface with cling film or dampened
greaseproof paper. Refrigerate.

Half an hour ahead

7 Cut off the stalks from the broccoli and cook them

in boiling salted water. As soon as they are tender add the florets and simmer for 4-5 minutes. Drain, reserving the cooking water.

To assemble

8 Reheat the sauce, stirring with a whisk, then mix in the broccoli and cheese.
9 Heat the oven to 400°F/200°C/Gas Mark 6. Arrange the potatoes in a nest on an ovenproof dish and bake for 5 minutes to reheat.
10 Pour the broccoli sauce into the centre and serve at once. Baked tomato halves can be cooked in the oven while reheating the potato shreds, and these are a good accompaniment to the main dish.

Hawaii Salad

QC ★ Serves 4-5
Takes about 30 minutes

1 large ripe pineapple
1 large orange
½ cucumber
¼ pint/140ml soured cream
2 tablespoons fresh lemon juice
8 cherry tomatoes
1 teaspoon raw cane sugar, granulated
¼ teaspoon sea salt
Centre leaves of 1 cos lettuce

1 Without removing the leaves rest the pineapple lengthwise on a wooden board. Using a sharp knife remove a thick slice the length of the pineapple. Cut the flesh from both the slice and the remaining pineapple, cut into cubes and put into a bowl.
2 Next remove all skin and pith from the orange and cut out the segments. Mix with the pineapple.
3 Peel and dice the cucumber. Mix with the orange and pineapple. Fold in the soured cream and lemon juice.
4 Quarter the tomatoes and sprinkle with sugar and salt. Line the larger section of pineapple skin with lettuce leaves. Fill with the fruit and vegetables, 'planting' the tomato quarters over the top. Cover with the pineapple lid.
5 Serve with wholemeal baps and rice salad.

Hazelnut and Celery Profiteroles with Hazelnut Sauce _____ PA ★ Serves 5-7

Wholemeal flour contains about one-fifth of its weight in bran. To lighten the pastry I sieve the flour before weighing and then use the bran in the filling. Baked unfilled buns can be frozen, enabling you to thaw only the number you estimate you will need.

Pastry

2 oz/55g plain white flour
3 oz/85g sieved wholemeal flour (about 3½ oz/100g before sieving)
Pinch sea salt
4 oz/115g butter
½ pint/285ml water
4 eggs

Filling/Sauce

2 celery sticks
2 oz/55g hazelnuts
1 oz/30g butter
1 oz/30g wholemeal flour
About 1 pint/570ml milk
Reserved bran
½ teaspoon ground mace
Sea salt
Freshly ground black pepper
Extra milk
1 oz/30g grated Leicester cheese (optional)

Optional Advance Preparations

About 1 month ahead

1 Sieve the white flour and sieved wholemeal flour and salt on to a sheet of greaseproof paper which will make it easier to shoot into the boiling water all at once.

2 Put the butter and water into a large saucepan and bring to the boil over moderate heat until the liquid rises up the sides of the pan. Immediately add all the flour and beat until the mixture leaves the sides of the pan.

3 Remove from the heat and continue beating for about 1 minute. Beat in the eggs one at a time. As each egg is added the mixture seems to separate and become globule-like but it will incorporate to a smooth glossy paste. Cover and leave until cold.

4 Grease and flour two large baking trays or line with non-stick vegetable parchment. Using two teaspoons place about twenty walnut-sized mounds of the paste, spread out on the baking trays.

5 Heat the oven to 425°F/220°C/Gas Mark 7 and bake the choux puffs for 15 minutes. Reduce the heat to 325°F/190°C/Gas Mark 5 for a further 10 minutes until the pastry has risen and is crisp and light brown.

6 Transfer the choux buns to a cooling wire and make slits in the sides to allow the steam to escape. When they are cold pack the buns carefully in a box and freeze.

Up to 1 month ahead

7 Make the sauce. Finely chop the celery and

hazelnuts and set the nuts aside. Sauté the celery in the butter until soft. Stir in the flour and cook for 1 minute.

8 Add the milk and cook, stirring continuously, until the sauce thickens. Add the bran reserved from the sieved flour and the mace and cook for a further 2 minutes. Season with salt and pepper.

9 Stir in the hazelnuts. Remove from the heat and cover with a disc of dampened greaseproof paper. Leave until cold, then freeze.

About 1 hour ahead

10 Remove the choux buns from the freezer and replace on a lined baking tray. Remove the sauce from the freezer and thaw and reheat gently in a saucepan or in the microwave.

11 Reserve half the mixture and purée the remainder in the liquidizer with sufficient milk to achieve a pouring consistency.

12 Heat the oven to 400°F/200°C/Gas Mark 6 and bake the choux buns for 5 minutes or until hot and re-crispened.

To assemble

13 Fill the centres of the hot choux buns with the chunky filling and arrange on a heated serving dish. Garnish with celery tops.

14 Reheat the smooth sauce, adjust the seasoning and stir in cheese if liked. Serve the sauce separately.

Hazelnut Steaks in Sorrel Sauce _____PA Serves 4

Country dwellers can usually obtain sorrel easily but if you are
unable to obtain it, substitute spinach. Shape the steaks any way
you please as they look attractive in the form of chops, but
understandably not all vegetarians would be happy with this idea.

Sauce

3½ oz/100g sorrel leaves
1½ oz/40g butter
½ pint/285ml single cream
1 oz/30g curd cheese
Sea salt
Freshly ground black pepper

Hazelnut Steaks

8 oz/225g shelled hazelnuts
8 oz/225g wholemeal bread or
breadcrumbs
8 oz/225g thawed or cooked
peas
2 eggs
Sea salt
Freshly ground black pepper

Optional Advance Preparations

Up to 24 hours ahead

1 Prepare the sauce. Rinse the sorrel leaves and pat
dry with a clean cloth.
2 Heat the butter in a heavy-based pan until
foaming. Stir in the sorrel and cook for 2 minutes,
stirring all the time. Add the cream and remove the
pan from the heat.
3 Purée the mixture in the blender, adding the
cheese, salt and pepper to taste. Leave to cool, then
cover and refrigerate.
4 Prepare the nutmeat steaks. Gradually feed all the
ingredients into the food processor, breaking the
bread into pieces as you go. This may be easier to do
in two batches. Adjust the seasoning to taste. The
mixture will be fairly stiff. Shape into steaks or cutlets
on a floured surface. Store, covered, in the refrigerator.

To assemble

5 Grill the steaks on an oiled foil-lined pan or lightly
fry for 5 minutes on each side.
6 Meanwhile heat the sauce over minimum heat or
in the microwave on the defrost setting.
7 Serve the steaks from a heated dish, garnished
with watercress sprigs, and hand the sauce separately.

Opposite *Courgette, Celery and Borlotti Salad (page 82)*
and *Salad Ufta Singh (page 124).*

Health Food Salad Bowl

NC Serves 4-5
Preparation time about 15 minutes

Serve with jacket potatoes if you have time to bake or microwave
them. Otherwise offer chunky wholemeal bread and unsalted
butter.

2 lettuce hearts
2 firm tomatoes
4 spring onions
2 hard-boiled eggs
2 avocados
4 tablespoons sunflower seeds
4 tablespoons cashew nuts
4 tablespoons mayonnaise (see
pages 29 or 37)
¼ pint/140ml buttermilk
Finely ground black pepper
1 handful beansprouts

1 Quarter the lettuce hearts. Slice the tomatoes. Trim
and slice the spring onions. Shell and coarsely chop
the eggs. Quarter, stone and slice the avocados.
2 Put all these ingredients into a large salad bowl
together with the seeds and nuts.
3 Mix the mayonnaise and buttermilk together and
add some black pepper. Fold into the salad items just
before serving and top with the beansprouts.

Hoisin Stir Fry

QC Serves 4-5
Takes about 25 minutes

Hoisin sauce is sold under the label of 'Barbecue' sauce. It has a
strong sweet flavour and makes a change from the ubiquitous soya
taste.

8 oz/225g French beans
8 oz/225g mange-tout
1 large carrot
1 bunch small spring onions
1 red pepper
1 green pepper
6 oz/170g wholewheat
spaghetti
½ oz/15g butter
1 tablespoon sesame oil
1 tablespoon hoisin sauce

1 First prepare the vegetables. Top and tail the beans
and mange-tout. Scrape the carrot. Cut into thin slices
lengthwise, then cut the slices into 1 inch/2.5cm strips.
2 Trim the spring onions and cut them into two or
three short lengths. Core, de-seed and cut the peppers
into thin strips.
3 Cook the spaghetti in plenty of boiling salted
water according to the directions on the packet.
4 Meanwhile heat the butter and oil in a sloping-
sided frying-pan until foaming. Toss in all the
vegetables and fry briskly for about 10 minutes,
stirring all the time, until the vegetables are just
tender. Stir in the hoisin sauce.
5 Tip the drained spaghetti on to a hot serving dish
and make a well in the middle. Fill with the hot
vegetables.

Opposite *Jewelled Crown (page 101).*

Hot Boursin Rolls_____PA ★ Serves 4-6

This is a good choice for serving as an after-theatre main course.

4-6 long wholemeal rolls
About 8oz/225g soft cream
garlic cheese
2 tomatoes
2-3 Chinese leaves
4-6 small field mushrooms
1 teaspoon sherry
Freshly ground black pepper
Butter
1 tablespoon sesame seeds

Optional Advance Preparations

Up to 24 hours ahead

1 Put the rolls on a work surface and make six or seven diagonal cuts not quite through to the bottom. Spread the cheese between the slices.
2 Slice the tomatoes and shred the Chinese leaves. Insert alternately into the cheese spread gaps.
3 Press the slices together and place the rolls on individual squares of foil. Wrap tightly, bringing up the sides of the foil to form a fold on top.

About 30 minutes ahead

4 Put the mushrooms in a shallow casserole dish in a single layer. Sprinkle with the sherry, some black pepper and a dab of butter. Put on to the top shelf of the oven.
5 Set the oven at 400°F/200°C/Gas Mark 6. Put the packets containing the rolls on a baking tray and bake for 10 minutes.

To assemble

6 Open up the foil. Sprinkle the tops with sesame seeds and bake for a further 5 minutes to crispen the tops.
7 Remove the rolls from the foil and serve with the mushrooms.

Hot Mushroom and Batavia Salad with Dijon Dressing

QC ★ Serves 4-5
Takes about 20 minutes

An average portion will be about 300 calories but slimmers can reduce this by using less oil.

1 Batavia lettuce
4 oz/115g Gouda cheese
1 lb/455g button mushrooms
1 oz/30g butter
1 garlic clove
4 tablespoons olive oil
1 tablespoon fresh lemon juice
1 teaspoon fresh tarragon leaves
2 tablespoons Dijon mustard
Sea salt
Freshly ground black pepper

1 Wash and drain the lettuce and tear into small pieces. Grate the cheese. Wipe the mushrooms.
2 Melt the butter in a frying-pan and sauté the mushrooms and garlic until the mushrooms are brown. Remove the garlic.
3 While the mushrooms are cooking put the oil, lemon juice, tarragon and mustard in a jar or jug and season sparingly with salt and pepper.
4 Toss the lettuce with the dressing and arrange on individual plates. Cover with a layer of grated cheese. Spoon the hot mushrooms on top.
5 Serve with a sheaf of freshly cooked French beans garnished with a plait of three fresh chives (see pages 24-5).

Hot Potato and Apple Salad

QC ★ Serves 4-5
Takes about 30 minutes

Baking potatoes can weigh up to ¾ lb/340g. The larger they are the less time need be spent on peeling them.

1 lb/455g large potatoes
Sea salt
2 medium onions
2 oz/55g butter
Freshly ground black pepper
3 dessert apples
2 teaspoons dark brown sugar
¼ teaspoon allspice
1 tablespoon Pernod
2 tablespoons chopped peanuts

1 Peel the potatoes and cut into ½ inch/1cm slices. Boil in salted water for 5 minutes or until just tender. Drain thoroughly.
2 Meanwhile peel and thinly slice the onions and sauté in half the butter until soft but not brown. Remove from the pan.
3 Add the remaining butter and some black pepper and fry the sliced potatoes a few at a time. Remove from the pan.
4 Wash, dry and core the apples and slice into rings. Add the sugar and spice to the juices left in the pan.
5 Raise the heat and turn the apple slices gently to coat with the syrup. Remove the apple slices from the syrup. Stir in the Pernod and nuts.
6 Arrange layers of potato, onion and apples in a warm serving dish.
7 Serve sprinkled with the Pernod and nut juices.

Imam Bayeldi

PA   Serves 6

Choose very small aubergines originating from Cyprus or Gambia and allow two per person. Left-over bayeldi can be eaten cold and will keep in the refrigerator for a day or two.

2 lb/900g aubergines
Sea salt
2 cloves garlic
Sunflower oil
1 large or 2 medium onions
2 lb/900g ripe tomatoes
Handful parsley sprigs
Freshly ground black pepper

Optional Advance Preparations

Up to 48 hours ahead

1 Rinse and dry the aubergines. Remove the stalks and cut in half lengthwise. Sprinkle the cut sides with salt and leave for 30 minutes. Rinse and drain well.
2 Crush the garlic well and spread over the aubergine halves. Heat about 1 inch/2.5cm oil in a large frying-pan or flameproof casserole and when hot fry the aubergines on both sides until brown. Remove the aubergines and drain on kitchen paper.

3 Slice the onions and chop the tomatoes. Drain most of the oil from the pan, then fry the onions and parsley. Stir in the tomatoes, plenty of pepper and salt to taste and simmer for about 10 minutes until the onions are soft.

4 Replace the aubergine halves in the frying-pan or transfer to a casserole.

Up to 1 hour ahead

5 Baste the aubergines with the sauce. Cover and cook gently for 20-30 minutes until the sauce is very thick.

To assemble

6 Serve with pitta bread or boiled rice and sliced hard-boiled eggs.

Jewelled Crown

NC   Serves 4-6
Takes 15 minutes plus chilling time

This small rice ring is deceptively filling. Try to cut the ring with two pastry servers to avoid spoiling the appearance of the individual servings.

1 small red pepper
1 small green pepper
1 small cucumber
3 tablespoons chick peas
3 tablespoons mayonnaise (see pages 29 or 37)
12 oz/340g cold cooked brown rice
6 tablespoons tomato purée
7 oz/200g tofu
1 teaspoon Holbrook's sauce
2 tablespoons double cream
Sea salt
Freshly ground black pepper
2 handfuls sprouted alfalfa

1 Core, seed and dice the peppers. Dice the cucumber.
2 Mix the diced vegetables, chick peas and mayonnaise with the rice. Pack into a 6 inch/15cm ring mould and refrigerate for one hour.
3 Meanwhile liquidize the tomato purée, tofu, Holbrook's sauce and cream until smooth. Season with salt and pepper. Turn the mould out on to a chilled serving dish. Surround with a border of alfalfa. Fill the centre of the rice ring with the purée.

Kashmiri Salad

Many vegetarians are also curry addicts. The chutney and curry
paste will keep for a very long time and can be used to flavour your
curries.

4 tablespoons cider vinegar
1 tablespoon sunflower oil
2 tablespoons aubergine
chutney
1 tablespoon mild curry paste
(see pages 32 or 33)
½ teaspoon sea salt
1 tablespoon chopped fresh
coriander leaves
2 oz/55g sultanas
1 small shallot
8 oz/225g white cabbage
3 oz/85g roast peanuts
1 dessert apple

1 Mix the vinegar, oil, chutney, curry paste, salt and
half the coriander leaves in a salad bowl. Stir in the
sultanas.
2 Peel and finely chop the shallot, shred the cabbage
and chop some of the peanuts. Quarter, core and
chop the apple.
3 Add all these ingredients to the salad bowl and
toss to coat them evenly. Sprinkle with the reserved
chopped coriander.
4 Serve with sliced chapattis or pitta bread and Raita
(see page 42).

Lamb's Lettuce and Mushroom Pâté Salad

Lamb's lettuces resemble tiny cos lettuces and are sweet, crisp and
fresh. They will keep for a day or two in a paper bag at the bottom
of the refrigerator.

8 oz/225g button mushrooms
1 bunch spring onions
2 oz/55g butter
2 tablespoons fresh chopped
parsley
1 teaspoon chopped sage leaves
1 tablespoon cornflour
3 tablespoons sherry
¼ pint/140ml soured cream
¼ pint/140ml yogurt
Sea salt
Freshly ground black pepper
Sage leaves to garnish
4 lamb's lettuces

Optional Advance Preparations

Up to 2 days ahead

1 Finely chop the mushrooms and the spring
onions. Put into a saucepan with the butter. Cook
gently for about 10 minutes, stirring from time to
time until the mushrooms are soft.
2 Mix in the parsley and sage. Blend the cornflour
with the sherry. Pour into the hot mushrooms and
cook, stirring continuously for a minute or two until
the mixture is thick.
3 Remove from the heat. Leave to cool, then cover
and refrigerate or freeze.

Up to 12 hours ahead

4 Remove from the freezer and leave to thaw. Beat in the soured cream and yogurt and season with salt and pepper.

To assemble

5 Spoon into a pâté dish and garnish with sage leaves. Arrange the lettuce leaves around a chilled serving platter and place the bowl in the middle.

Linguine with Walnut Sauce

QC ★ Serves 4-5
Takes about 20 minutes

Fresh basil makes all the difference to the sauce, giving it an authentic Italian flavour.

2 teacups fresh basil
1 garlic clove
3 oz/85g shelled refreshed walnuts (pages 23-4)
1 oz/30g grated Parmesan cheese
About 7 fl oz/200ml first pressing olive oil
½ oz/15g salted butter
1 teaspoon tomato paste
1 lb/455g flat linguine
Extra Parmesan

1 To make the sauce speedily, put the basil, garlic, pine nuts and cheese in the blender and process until smooth. Add the oil a little at a time until it has absorbed as much as it can (after this point is reached, the oil forms a thin layer on the surface).
2 Now add the butter and tomato paste and process briefly. Add salt only if necessary.
3 Cook the pasta in boiling salted water. Drain until the cooking water just stops dripping, then mix in half the sauce.
4 Pour the remaining sauce over individual portions and add an extra sprinkling of Parmesan.
5 Serve with a salad of raddichio and green lettuce.

Market Harborough Salad with Cheese Twigs _____PA ★ Serves 4-5

Endives are always on the large side. The outside leaves are bitter but the heart is crisp and fresh.

Cheese Twigs

2 oz/55g plain white flour
1 oz/30g wholemeal flour
2 oz/55g butter
2 oz/55g grated Cheddar cheese
Freshly ground black pepper
Cayenne

Salad

4 tablespoons cooked butter beans
8 oz/225g fresh young spinach
5 oz/140g raddichio
1 endive heart
2 small onions
2 eggs
3 tablespoons sesame oil
1 tablespoon fresh lemon juice
Sea salt
Freshly ground black pepper

Optional Advance Preparations

Up to 1 month ahead

1 Make the cheese twigs. Sift the flours into a mixing bowl. Rub in the butter to form large sticky crumbs. Stir in the cheese. Season with pepper and cayenne.
2 Knead to a manageable dough. Chill for ½ hour. Roll out on a floured surface to ¼ inch/5mm thickness. Cut into twenty 3×½ inch/7.5×1cm strips.
3 Spread out on a baking tray. Twist the strips at either end. Chill again for 30 minutes.
4 Bake in a preheated oven 350°F/180°C/Gas Mark 4 until crisp (about 15 minutes).
5 Leave until cool before removing from the baking tray. Store in an airtight container.

Up to 4 days ahead

6 Cook the butter beans unless using tinned beans (see page 21).

Up to 24 hours ahead

7 Wash and spin the spinach, raddichio and endive. Pile the spinach leaves on top of one another and slice thinly. Tear the larger raddichio leaves into pieces. Cut the endive into sprigs.
8 Peel and thinly slice the onions and separate the rings.
9 Put all the salad ingredients into a plastic box lined with kitchen paper to absorb any surplus moisture. Tightly put on the lid and store in the bottom of the refrigerator.
10 Boil, cool, shell and chop the eggs and refrigerate in a covered dish.
11 Mix the oil, lemon juice, salt and pepper in a bottle or jar. Cover and set aside.

To assemble

12 Transfer the salad ingredients to a large bowl and mix in the beans. Just before serving beat the dressing throughly to mix, pour over the salad and gently toss the salad with two large spoons. Sprinkle with the egg and serve cheese straws separately.

Moroccan Salad _____ PA ★ Serves 4-6

6 dry chestnuts
6 oz/170g brown rice
Sea salt
2 tablespoons sunflower oil
1 tablespoon olive oil
1 tablespoon red wine vinegar
½ teaspoon ground coriander
¼ teaspoon freshly ground black pepper
2 oz/55g sultanas
8 large tomatoes
¼ cucumber
1 escarole lettuce

Optional Advance Preparations

Up to 2 months ahead

1 Soak the chestnuts overnight, drain and rinse. Cook the rice and chestnuts together in plenty of boiling salted water.

2 Drain and coarsely chop the chestnuts with kitchen scissors. Stir in the oils, vinegar, coriander, pepper and sultanas. Cool, cover and freeze.

Up to 24 hours ahead

3 Transfer to the refrigerator to thaw.

Up to 12 hours ahead

4 Cut a slice from the stalk end of each tomato. Set aside. Scoop the tomato centres into a bowl. Chop with scissors.

5 Finely dice and add the cucumber. Stir in the rice mixture. Fill the tomato shells with the mixture. Arrange on a bed of shredded lettuce. Replace the tomato lids.

To assemble

6 Arrange the lettuce leaves over a serving platter and place the tomatoes on the lettuce.

Mushrooms Budapest

A light supper dish that could be served as a starter for eight
people.

*8 oz/225g short grain brown
rice
Sea salt
1 lb/455g mushrooms
1 small onion
1 oz/30g butter
1 teaspoon paprika
¼ pint/140ml double cream
2 tablespoons cornflour
Freshly ground black pepper*

1 Put the rice into a saucepan, adding ½ teaspoon
salt and 1 pint/570ml cold water. Bring to the boil.
2 Stir, then reduce the heat and simmer covered for
25 minutes or until the rice is tender and the water is
absorbed.
3 Meanwhile finely slice the mushrooms. Peel and
finely chop the onion.
4 Put the butter and onion in a saucepan and sauté,
stirring frequently until the onion is soft. Stir in the
paprika and mushrooms.
5 Cover the lid and cook gently for 10 minutes or
until the mushrooms are tender.
6 Pour the cream into a jug and blend in the
cornflour. Stir into the mushrooms. Bring to the boil.
Season with salt and pepper.
7 Turn the hot rice into a serving dish and pour the
mushrooms on top. Serve with steamed broccoli.

Mushrooms in Vermouth

You will need two large saucepans to cook this. If you use pre-
cooked rice it can be reheated in a microwave or by dropping it in a
saucepan of boiling water.

*8 oz/225g long-grain brown
rice
1 vegetable stock cube
1 tablespoon freshly chopped
parsley
1 lb/455g button mushrooms
2 oz/55g butter
1 teaspoon Holbrook's sauce
Freshly ground black pepper
5 tablespoons vermouth*

1 Cook the rice in about ¾ pint/425ml water with
the vegetable stock cube and parsley.
2 Once the rice has been put on to cook, prepare the
mushrooms. Wipe and toss them in a clean cloth.
3 Heat the butter in a large pan and sauté the
mushrooms until lightly brown. Stir in the
Holbrook's sauce and black pepper.
4 Add the vermouth and cook for 5 minutes to
drive off the alcohol and reduce the juices.
5 Serve the mushrooms hot on a bed of rice.

Mushroom Pielets

The average content in a 15 oz/425g tin of beans is 10 oz/285g.

6 oz/170g button mushrooms
2 tomatoes
10 oz/285g cooked butter
beans
1 oz/30g butter
1 tablespoon fresh lemon juice
1 tablespoon tomato purée
Dash Holbrook's sauce
Sea salt
Freshly ground black pepper
2 oz/55g fresh wholemeal
breadcrumbs
1 oz/30g grated Cheddar
cheese
1 tablespoon freshly chopped
parsley

1 Chop the mushrooms. Skin and chop the tomatoes. Mash the beans.

2 Melt the butter and sauté the mushrooms and tomatoes until the mushrooms are just tender.

3 Stir in the beans, lemon juice, tomato purée and Holbrook's sauce. Add a little salt and plenty of black pepper.

4 Cook for a minute or two to heat the beans. Spoon into flameproof ramekins or scallop shells.

5 Mix the breadcrumbs, cheese and parsley together and sprinkle on top. Brown under a hot grill.

6 Serve hot with a crisp green salad.

Oeufs Sous les Draps

This is a pleasant recipe to grace an elegant table.

8 oz/225g potatoes
1 lb/455g young leeks
4 eggs
1 oz/30g butter
1 oz/30g wholemeal flour
½ teaspoon mustard powder
½ pint/285ml milk
4 oz/115g grated Leicester cheese
Sea salt
Freshly ground black pepper
Parsley sprigs to garnish

1 Peel and dice the potatoes. Wash and chop the leeks. Put into a large pan of boiling salted water.
2 Add the eggs in their shells and cook for 15 minutes until the vegetables are soft. Remove and shell the eggs and halve lengthways. Drain the vegetables.
3 Meanwhile, using a second saucepan melt the butter. Stir in the flour and mustard, then blend in the milk. Cook over moderate heat, stirring continuously, until the sauce thickens, then cook for a further 2 minutes.
4 Stir in half the cheese and season with salt and pepper.
5 Place a bed of leeks and potatoes in a shallow flameproof dish. Arrange the eggs round-side up on the vegetables.
6 Pour the sauce evenly over the eggs and sprinkle with the remaining cheese. Brown under a medium grill.
7 Garnish with parsley sprigs.

Okra and Tomato Hot Pot

QC Serves 4-5
Takes about 30 minutes

In vegetarian cookery it is difficult to obtain the glutinous texture of
meat sauces. Okra is one of the few vegetables to provide a similar
result.

1 lb/455g fresh firm okra
1 medium onion
1 green pepper
1 oz/30g butter
1½ lb/680g tomatoes or
1 large and 1 small tin
chopped tomatoes
1 tablespoon dried basil
Sea salt
Freshly ground black pepper
3 tablespoons sweet red wine
2 tablespoons flaked almonds

1 Rinse, top and tail the okra. Peel and finely chop
the onion. Core, seed and dice the green pepper.
2 Melt the butter in a flameproof casserole or
attractive sauté pan and gently fry the onion and
pepper for 5 minutes.
3 Add the okra and cook for another 5 minutes
until the okra begins to soften.
4 Chop the tomatoes and add to the pan with the
basil and season with salt and pepper.
5 Cover with the lid and simmer for 10 minutes,
then remove the lid, add the wine and bring to the
boil.
6 While the vegetables are cooking spread the
almonds on foil and brown under the grill.
7 Sprinkle the nuts over the hot pot and serve with
Lyonnaise potatoes and Brussels sprouts.

Pakora

An excellent batter can be made using besan flour and water alone.
Left-overs can be frozen and reheated in a hot oven.

6 oz/170g besan flour
About 7 fl oz/200ml cold
water
About 2 teaspoons garam
masala
Sea salt
3 medium onions
2 medium courgettes
1 small aubergine
8 cauliflower florets
Oil for deep frying

1 Put the besan flour into a large bowl and add sufficient cold water to achieve a very thick batter. Stir in the garam masala and a little salt.
2 Peel the onions and cut each into four wedges. Top, tail and cut the courgettes into 1 inch/2.5cm chunks. Peel and cut up the aubergine.
3 Heat a pan of salted water and when boiling add all the vegetables. Bring back to the boil and cook for 5 minutes. Drain thoroughly.
4 Stir the vegetables into the batter. Pour about 1 inch/2.5cm oil in a deep saucepan and fry the vegetables on all sides a few at a time.
5 Remove them with a slotted spoon and drain on kitchen paper. Pile into a large wooden bowl and serve hot. A green side salad and Raita (see page 42) go very well with Pakora.

Palm Hearts St Jacques

Salsify can be used instead of palm hearts but they discolour as
soon as they are scraped.

1-1½ lb/455-680g large
potatoes
1 oz/30g butter
2 tablespoons milk
Sea salt
Freshly ground black pepper
1 large tin palm hearts
2 tablespoons soft margarine
3 tablespoons flour
¼ pint/140ml white wine
¼ teaspoon lemon juice
¼ pint/140ml single cream

Optional Advance Preparations

Up to 24 hours ahead

1 Boil the potatoes in salted water until well cooked. Drain thoroughly and mash with the butter and milk and season with salt and pepper.
2 Put the potato into a piping bag, fitted with a ½ inch/1cm nozzle and pipe a border of potato around the edges of individual scallop shells or dishes.
3 Drain the palm hearts and cut into 1 inch/2.5cm lengths. Blend the margarine and flour together in a small bowl.
4 Heat the wine and lemon juice together in a

frying-pan. When the liquid is boiling beat in the paste a little at a time, stirring continuously. Season with salt and pepper.

15 minutes before serving

5 Put the palm hearts in the sauce and cook for 2-3 minutes until hot.

To assemble

6 Place the palm hearts in the prepared dishes. Stir the cream into the sauce and pour over them. Put under a hot grill to brown the potato.

Pancakes Blé Noir with Cream Cheese and Mustard Filling

QC Serves 6
Takes about 35 minutes

Pancakes made with buckwheat flour are a speciality in Brittany. They are darker and heavier than traditional 'crêpes' but have a delicious nutty flavour and can become quite addictive. Buckwheat pancakes can be stacked and frozen to be reheated and stuffed with a variety of fillings. Make a double quantity therefore if you wish.

Pancakes

2 oz/55g buckwheat flour
3 oz/85g plain white flour
1 tablespoon baking powder
½ teaspoon sea salt
1 tablespoon molasses (or dark treacle)
4 tablespoons sunflower oil
1 egg
8 fl oz/225ml warm milk

Filling

12 oz/340g cream cheese
6 tablespoons horseradish sauce
1 teaspoon made-up English mustard
Dash Tabasco
2 oz/55g almond flakes

1 First make the filling. Beat the cheese, horseradish sauce, mustard and Tabasco together and set aside.
2 Sieve the flours, baking powder and salt into a mixing bowl.
3 Beat in the molasses, oil, egg and milk. Set aside for 10 minutes until bubbly. Beat once more.
4 Fry the pancakes in a non-stick frying-pan or in a lightly-oiled ordinary pan one at a time. The mixture should make six.
5 Spread some cheese mixture over one half of each pancake. Place the folded pancakes in a single layer in a flameproof dish.
6 Spread with the remaining cheese and flaked almonds. Heat quickly under the grill. Serve at once with a green salad.

Parsleyed Potatoes with Courgette and Red Wine Casserole

QC   Serves 4-6
Takes about 35 minutes

Potatoes cook well in the pressure cooker and this could reduce the cooking time to 5 minutes.

1½ lb/680g tiny new potatoes
Sea salt
1 oz/30g butter or margarine
3 tablespoons freshly chopped parsley
Freshly ground black pepper
1½ lb/680g courgettes, rinsed
2 tablespoons walnut oil
8 oz/225g tin tomatoes
2 tablespoons tomato purée
4 tablespoons medium red wine
¼ teaspoon garlic salt
¼ teaspoon ground allspice
1 teaspoon cornflour
2 oz/55g grated Edam cheese
1 tablespoon grated Parmesan cheese

1 Wash the potatoes but do not skin. Cook in boiling salted water for about 20 minutes until tender. Drain.

2 Return the potatoes to the saucepan. Stir in the butter and parsley and season with some black pepper. Switch off the heat. Cover to keep warm.

3 While the potatoes are cooking, top, tail and thinly slice the courgettes.

4 Heat the oil in a frying-pan and sauté the courgettes for about 5 minutes until golden.

5 Stir in the tomatoes, tomato purée, wine, garlic salt, ground allspice and cornflour.

6 Cook for 3 minutes. Stir in the grated Edam cheese, then pour into a shallow greased casserole. Sprinkle with the Parmesan.

7 Bake at 400°F/200°C/Gas Mark 6 for 15 minutes or until crispening on top. Serve with the potatoes.

Pasta Napoletana

Takes 25-30 minutes depending on the type of pasta used

Fresh pasta will cook in a minute or two and can be purchased
from larger supermarkets.

2 cloves garlic
1×14 oz/400g tin tomatoes
2 tablespoons tomato purée
½ teaspoon dried basil
Pinch sugar
¼ pint/140ml dry red wine
Sea salt
Freshly ground black pepper
6 oz/170g Mozzarella
2 teaspoons salad oil
4 oz/115g wholemeal pasta
4 oz/115g green pasta strips

1 Peel and finely slice the garlic and put into a large
pan with the tomatoes, tomato purée, basil and sugar.
2 Bring to the boil, lower the heat and simmer for 10
minutes, stirring frequently to prevent burning. Dice
the Mozzarella.
3 Add the wine and cook until hot, then season
with salt and pepper. Add the Mozzarella. Stir until
melted. Cover and keep warm.
4 Bring two large pans of salted water to the boil,
add a teaspoon of oil to each and cook the
wholemeal and green pasta separately.
5 Drain in a colander, pouring the wholemeal pasta
through one side and the green pasta through the
other.
6 Arrange a circle of green pasta on a hot serving
dish, place the wholemeal pasta in the centre.
7 Reheat the sauce, pour half over the pasta and
serve the remaining sauce separately.

Pear and Cheddar Salad

Takes about 15 minutes

1 small orange
¼ pint/140ml natural yogurt
2 tablespoons walnut oil
Sea salt
Freshly ground black pepper
1 celery stick
2 oz/55g Cheddar cheese
4 ripe but firm pears
2 tablespoons lemon juice
1 bunch watercress

1 Squeeze the juice of the orange into a large bowl
and stir in the yogurt, walnut oil and salt and pepper
to taste.
2 Finely chop the celery. Dice the cheese.
3 Rinse, dry, core and cut up three pears and fold
into the salad. Peel, quarter and core the remaining
pear and cut each section lengthwise. Soak in the
lemon juice.
4 Rinse and trim the watercress, coarsely chop and
put in a wooden salad bowl. Spoon the salad on to
the watercress.
5 Garnish with a fan of pear wedges.

Poached Eggs Champenoise

QC   Serves 4
Takes about 15 minutes

Boiling the wine drives off the alcohol but increases the flavour.
Choose the driest wine obtainable.

4 thick slices wholemeal bread
1 pint/570ml sparkling white
wine
4 eggs
5 tablespoons double cream
Sea salt
Freshly ground black pepper
Sprigs of fresh thyme

1 Toast the bread and keep warm.
2 Pour all but 2 tablespoons of the wine into a shallow frying-pan. Bring to the boil, then reduce the heat and simmer until only one quarter of the wine remains.
3 Break in the eggs; try to keep them separate. Cover the pan with a lid and poach for about 2 minutes. When the eggs are lightly cooked remove them with a fish slice or slotted spoon and place on the toast.
4 Stir the cream into the small quantity of hot wine left in the pan. Replace over the heat and without covering fast boil until reduced to a thick cream. At first the sauce will seem to thin but subsequently thickens to a rich dark syrup.
5 Season with salt and pepper. Mix in the reserved wine and immediately pour over the eggs.
6 Garnish with a sprig of thyme.

Pommes Soufflé with Watercress Purée ____PA Serves 4-5

A really delicious dish which is more substantial than the usual soufflé.

2 lb/900g potatoes, peeled
½ teaspoon powdered saffron
2 oz/55g butter
2 eggs, separated plus 2 egg whites
About ½ pint/285ml milk
2 tablespoons grated Edam cheese
Sea salt
Freshly ground black pepper

Watercress Purée

3 bunches watercress
7 fl oz/200ml hot water
½ vegetable stock cube
½ oz/15g butter
½ oz/15g wholemeal flour

Optional Advance Preparations

About 24 hours ahead of time

1 Dice and cut up and boil the potatoes in lightly salted water to which you have added the saffron. Drain and mash the potatoes with the butter.
2 Add the beaten egg yolks and sufficient milk to arrive at the consistency of half-whipped cream. Stir in the cheese and season with salt and freshly ground black pepper.
3 Using clean beaters whisk the four egg whites to soft peaks. Fold into the potato mixture and turn into a lightly greased 2½ pint/1.5 litre soufflé dish. Cover and refrigerate.

Up to 24 hours ahead of time

4 Rinse the watercress, remove the tough stems and put the trimmed watercress in a saucepan with the water and crumble in the stock cube. Bring to the boil.
5 Meanwhile blend the butter and flour together. Add a little at a time to the boiling watercress and beat thoroughly. Continue cooking over a moderate heat for about 5 minutes.
6 Cover the surface of the sauce with dampened greaseproof paper and refrigerate when cool.
Although the sauce can be prepared ahead, it can also be made fresh whilst the soufflé is baking.

To assemble

7 Preheat the oven to 400°F/200°C/Gas Mark 6, then bake the soufflé in the centre of the oven for 20-25 minutes until well risen and brown.
8 Reheat the purée if necessary, adding a little milk or water. Heat the dinner plates and serve the hot soufflé immediately it comes from the oven. Pour the purée over individual portions.

Provençale Crumble _____PA ★ Serves 5-6

The flavour is obtained by frying the vegetables before casserolling.
Slimmers could omit pre-frying the aubergine and courgette.

2 oz/55g butter
3 oz/85g wholemeal flour
½ oz/15g rye flakes
1 tablespoon grated Parmesan
1 teaspoon chopped basil
1 large onion
2 green peppers
1 garlic clove
1 large aubergine
2 medium courgettes
Sea salt
About ¼ pint/140ml
sunflower oil
1 lb/455g tomatoes
Handful parsley sprigs
Freshly ground black pepper

Optional Advance Preparations

Up to 2 months ahead

1 Rub the butter into the flour until it resembles large breadcrumbs. Chop and add the rye flakes, the Parmesan cheese and basil. Freeze in a covered container.

2 Peel and slice the onion. Core, de-seed and dice the peppers. Peel and crush the garlic and set all aside.

3 Rinse the aubergine and slice thinly. Top and tail the courgettes and slice thinly. Put into a colander over a large bowl and sprinkle generously with salt and then cover with a plate. Leave for one hour. Rinse and drain well. Pat dry with kitchen paper.

4 Heat a few tablespoons of oil in a large frying-pan and fry the aubergine and courgettes, a few slices at a time, until they are golden. Remove and drain each batch, adding extra oil as necessary.

5 When all the aubergine and courgettes are cooked, lightly sauté the garlic, onions and peppers. When these vegetables are tender, quarter and add the tomatoes and continue cooking for about 5 minutes. Stir in the parsley and season with salt and pepper.

6 Layer the aubergine and courgettes and the other sautéed vegetables in a casserole. Leave until cool, then cover and freeze.

About 2 hours ahead

7 Remove the vegetable casserole and crumb topping from the freezer. Sprinkle the topping over the vegetables.

To assemble

8 Bake the dish in a moderately hot oven 375°F/190°C/Gas Mark 5 for 45 minutes or until the filling is hot and the crumble mix brown.

Quenelles en Robe

Little poached cheese and almond dumplings with a tomato sauce.

Sauce

1 oz/30g butter
1 oz/30g wholemeal flour
14 fl oz/400ml milk
1 tablespoon chervil
3 tablespoons tomato purée
Sea salt
Freshly ground black pepper

Quenelles

¼ pint/140ml water
1 oz/30g butter
Sea salt
Freshly ground black pepper
2 oz/55g wholemeal flour
2 eggs
1 oz/30g ground almonds
3 oz/85g Cheddar cheese, grated
¼ teaspoon mustard powder
Watercress to garnish

1 To make the sauce, melt the butter in a saucepan over moderate heat. Stir in the flour. Add the milk and chervil. Bring to the boil, stirring continuously.

2 Reduce the heat and continue cooking for about 2 minutes. Add the tomato purée and salt and pepper to taste.

3 To make the quenelles, put the water, butter and a pinch of salt and pepper in a saucepan. Bring to the boil over moderate heat so that the butter has a chance to melt.

4 Immediately toss in the flour and beat vigorously until the mixture leaves the sides of the pan. Remove from the heat.

5 Add 1 egg and beat until it is fully incorporated. Add the second egg and beat until the mixture is of a smooth consistency. Beat in the ground almonds, cheese, mustard powder and seasoning.

6 Bring a large pan of salted water to a full rolling boil. Add the mixture a tablespoon at a time, well spaced to allow for swelling. Cook on the boil for 3 minutes. Remove with a slotted spoon and transfer to a heated serving dish.

7 To serve, coat the quenelles with the sauce and garnish with watercress leaves.

117

Red Salad

The thick stem should be removed from the cabbage as it is
indigestible to eat raw.

2 small raddichio lettuces
8 oz/225g red cabbage
2 medium tomatoes
1 medium beetroot
5 tablespoons mayonnaise (see
pages 29 or 37)
6 ready-to-eat pitted prunes
12 small radishes
2 tablespoons finely chopped
hazelnuts

1 Wash the raddichio, cabbage and tomatoes and
dry well. Arrange the raddichio leaves on individual
plates.
2 Finely grate the cabbage. Grate the beetroot.
3 Liquidize the tomatoes with the mayonnaise and
prunes. Mix in a large bowl with the cabbage. Pile on
to the raddichio.
4 Garnish with the radishes and sprinkle with the
nuts.

Ribbon Grill

PA   Serves 4

Almost a meal in one dish. A green side salad is the only
accompaniment necessary.

4 oz/115g kidney beans
4 oz/115g yellow split peas
½ oz/15g butter
1 teaspoon turmeric
Sea salt
Freshly ground black pepper
1 lb/455g potatoes
2 tablespoons milk
8 oz/225g fresh or frozen peas
8 oz/225g cream cheese

Optional Advance Preparations

Up to 5 days ahead

1 Soak and cook the kidney beans (boiling them).
Drain, cool and store covered in the refrigerator or
freezer.
2 Rinse and cook the split peas in plenty of water.
Drain and mash with the butter and turmeric.
Season with salt and pepper. Cool and store in the
refrigerator or freezer.

Up to 24 hours ahead

3 Peel and boil the potatoes. Drain and mash with
the milk, adding salt and pepper to taste.

45 minutes ahead

4 Cook the peas and drain.

To assemble

5 In a rectangular flameproof casserole dish arrange
the beans, split peas, peas and potatoes in four strips.

6 Cover the beans, split peas and the other peas, but not the potatoes with spoonsful of the cheese.

7 Place the dish under a medium grill until the cheese spreads, then raise the heat and cook for about 10 minutes until browned.

Rice Darioles with Walnut Sauce on Carrot Rings

QC ★ Serves 4
Takes about 45 minutes

Dariole moulds are well worth buying — they are about 2 inches/5cm tall and when the food is turned out it is 'sandcastle' shaped. It is not necessary to buy several as they can be filled and turned out quickly. Ramekins can be substituted but the effect is not so good.

6 oz/170g short-grain brown rice
1 vegetable stock cube
1 lb/455g young even-sized carrots
Sea salt
½ teaspoon salad oil
3 oz/85g shelled walnuts
1 thick slice wholemeal bread
8 oz/225g Quark or similar low-fat soft cheese
2 tablespoons grated Parmesan cheese
2 tablespoons chopped chives
¼ teaspoon garlic salt
Freshly ground black pepper

1 Cook the rice according to the directions on the packet, adding the stock cube to the water. While the rice is cooking lightly grease four dariole moulds if you have that number.

2 Trim and scrape the carrots and slice thickly. Place in a saucepan and just cover with water. Add a little salt and the oil. Bring to the boil, then reduce the heat. Cover with a tightly fitting lid and simmer for about 10 minutes.

3 To prepare the sauce, purée the walnuts, bread (roughly torn), Quark, Parmesan and chives together and add garlic salt and pepper to taste. Pour into a saucepan.

4 When the rice is ready, drain the carrots, adding about 4 tablespoons of the cooking water to the sauce. Set the sauce to heat gently but do not allow to boil.

5 Meanwhile arrange the carrots on individual plates. Fill the dariole moulds with the rice, pressing well down, then turn out the 'castles' on to the carrots. Pour the sauce over the rice and serve hot.

Sabzi Bhajis

A choice of whole spice or creamy curry for three vegetables cooked
separately. Together they will serve four to eight persons. Curry
freezes well but will keep for about 2 days under refrigeration.
Always store well covered to prevent the pungent flavour from
affecting other foods. If time is not important cook consecutively in
the same pan and keep hot.

Green Beans Bhajis
1½ lb/680g French beans
¼ pint/140ml curry base (see
pages 32 or 33)
1 tablespoon tomato purée
4 fl oz/60ml water
¼ teaspoon sea salt
¼ teaspoon freshly ground
black pepper
1 tablespoon freshly chopped
coriander leaves

1 Top and tail the beans and cook in boiling water
for 5 minutes to part cook.
2 Heat the curry base in a heavy-based saucepan
over low heat. Stir in the tomato purée, water, salt
and some black pepper.
3 Add the coriander and beans and cook over
moderate heat, stirring occasionally, for 5-6 minutes
or until the water is absorbed.

Aloo Tikha

1½ lb/680g potatoes
¼ pint/140ml curry base (see
pages 32 or 33)
1 tablespoon soya sauce
½ teaspoon freshly ground
black pepper
½ teaspoon sea salt
1 tablespoon freshly chopped
coriander leaves

1 Peel the potatoes and cut into bite-sized cubes. Boil in salted water for 5 minutes to half cook. Drain, reserving the water.
2 Put the curry base in a heavy-based saucepan over low heat and add 4-5 tablespoons of potato water or plain water, soya sauce, pepper, salt and coriander and cook for a further 2-3 minutes until well blended. Fold in the potatoes, raise the heat and stir fry for 5-7 minutes or until the potatoes are lightly browned and coated in the curry base.

Cauliflower Bhaji

1 large cauliflower
1 tablespoon sunflower oil
6 green peppercorns
6 whole green cardamoms
½ teaspoon turmeric
¼ pint/140ml curry base (see
pages 32 or 33)
5 tablespoons defrosted frozen
peas
2 fl oz/60ml vegetable stock or
water
½ teaspoon sea salt
1 tablespoon freshly chopped
coriander leaves
¼ teaspoon freshly ground
black pepper

1 Wash the cauliflower and divide into florets.
2 Heat the oil over medium heat. Add the peppercorns and cardamoms and fry for 30 seconds until they start to pop.
3 Stir in the turmeric, then add the cauliflower florets and fry briskly for 2 minutes to brown the edges and give a yellow tinge.
4 Mix in the curry base, peas and stock or water. Stir well, then cover and simmer over low heat for 10 minutes.
5 Remove the lid, raise the heat and continue cooking until the water is completely absorbed and the cauliflower is cooked but still retains its crisp texture.
6 Garnish with salt, coriander and pepper.

Salade du Soleil

An attractive fruity salad which can be adapted to include most
juicy fruits.

1 lb/455g large carrots
2 tablespoons large seedless
raisins
2 thick slices fresh pineapple
1 small red pepper
2 oz/55g Feta cheese
3 tablespoons French dressing
¼ teaspoon French mustard
1 tablespoon single cream
Freshly ground black pepper
Small bunch seedless grapes
2 tablespoons roast millet
flakes

1 Peel the carrots and cut in half crosswise, then cut
each piece lengthwise into matchsticks.
2 Place with the raisins in a saucepan and just cover
with water. Bring to the boil, cool in a colander under
cold running water and leave to drain.
3 Dice the pineapple. De-seed and dice the red
pepper. Dice the Feta cheese.
4 Beat the French dressing, mustard and cream
together and season with some black pepper.
5 In a salad bowl mix the carrot strips, raisins,
pineapple, red pepper and cheese. Fold in the
dressing.
6 Serve decorated with the grapes and millet flakes.

Salad International

White rice is best in this recipe. The lentils and nuts add extra
goodness.

2 oz/55g red lentils
8 oz/225g long-grain rice
1 green pepper
4 spring onions
12 stuffed green olives
1 tin artichoke hearts
1 tin water chestnuts
About 8 tablespoons
mayonnaise (see pages 29
or 37)
About 1 teaspoon curry
powder
1 tablespoon fresh lemon juice
1 tablespoon cashew nuts

Optional Advance Preparations

Up to 3 days ahead

1 Wash and pick over the lentils, then soak for a few
hours. Drain and boil in fresh water for about 20
minutes. Drain well and when cool refrigerate
covered.
2 Cook the rice in plenty of salted water in a
saucepan or the microwave for about 15 minutes or
until just tender. Drain through a colander and rinse
under cold running water. Leave to drain until cool,
then refrigerate, loosely covered, or freeze if preferred.

Up to 24 hours ahead

3 Core, seed and chop the pepper. Trim and finely
slice the spring onions. Slice the olives. Drain the
artichoke hearts, reserving the liquid.

4 Drain and slice the water chestnuts. Mix the mayonnaise and curry powder together and gently stir into the vegetables. Cover and refrigerate.

Half an hour before serving

5 Mix the rice and lentils together with the lemon juice and 1 tablespoon of the reserved artichoke liquor.

To assemble

6 Spoon on to a serving dish. Top with the vegetables and a sprinkling of chopped cashew nuts.

Salad Elizabeth _____ PA ★ Serves 4

Only one half of an iceberg lettuce is needed in this recipe but since it is a lettuce variety that keeps for a few days, there need be no waste.

4 oz/115g long-grain brown rice
1 tablespoon safflower oil
1 tablespoon fresh lemon juice
2 teaspoons French mustard
¼ teaspoon garlic salt
Pinch ground ginger
¼ teaspoon freshly ground black pepper
½ iceberg lettuce
¼ cucumber
4 oz/115g cottage cheese
2 tablespoons finely chopped chives

Optional Advance Preparations

Up to 3 days ahead

1 Cook the rice according to the directions on the packet, cover and refrigerate. Cooked rice freezes well for 2 or 3 months.

2 Combine the oil, lemon juice, mustard, garlic salt, ginger and pepper in a sealed bottle.

Up to 2 hours ahead

3 Shred the lettuce. Cut the cucumber into 1 inch/2.5cm thick slices, then cut each into matchsticks.

To assemble

4 Arrange the lettuce on a serving dish. Mix the rice with the dressing and spread over the lettuce.

5 Pile the cottage cheese and chives in the centre and surround with the cucumber sticks. A slightly quicker alternative is to buy the cottage cheese and chives already mixed.

Salad Ufta Singh _____ PA ★ Serves 6

A curried wholewheat, mushroom and sweetcorn salad with a
tropical fruit topping, which could be increased with very little
extra effort to serve as a buffet party dish.

6 oz/170g wholewheat grains
8 oz/225g open field
mushrooms
1 oz/30g butter
1 tablespoon mild curry paste
3 oz/85g cooked sweetcorn
(tinned or frozen)
1 oz/30g cashew nuts
¼ pint/140ml natural yogurt
1 tablespoon sunflower oil
Sea salt
Freshly ground black pepper
1 large ripe mango
8 oz/225g fresh lychees or
small tin well rinsed to remove
the sweetness
Juice of 2 small limes

Optional Advance Preparations

Up to 1 month ahead

1 Cook the wheat grains in plenty of water for about
one hour or until they are tender. Drain, cover and
refrigerate for 2 days or freeze for up to one month.

24 hours ahead

2 Slice the mushrooms and sauté in the butter for
about 5 minutes until just cooked, but not soft. Stir
in the curry paste. Leave to cool down, then mix in
the wheat and sweetcorn.

3 Chop and add the cashew nuts. Stir in the yogurt
and oil. Season with salt and pepper. Cover and
refrigerate.

About 2 hours ahead

4 Peel, slice and then cut up the mango. Peel and
stone the lychees. Sprinkle the lime juice on the fruit
and toss carefully.

To assemble

5 Stir the refrigerated salad and put into a serving
dish. Top with the mango and lychees.

Salade d'Olives Noires

The ingredients are simple and easy to obtain. Try to buy pitted
olives and then your guests will not have the problem of removing
stones from their mouths discreetly.

1 lb/455g small firm tomatoes
3 hard-boiled eggs
1 small bunch spring onions
4 oz/115g black olives
1 tablespoon olive oil
1 teaspoon red wine vinegar
Sea salt
Freshly ground black pepper
2 tablespoons mayonnaise (see
pages 29 or 37)

1 Slice the tomatoes. Shell and slice the eggs. Trim
and finely slice the spring onions.
2 On individual plates arrange a border of tomato
and egg slices alternately. Fill the centre with spring
onions and top with the olives.
3 Mix the oil, vinegar, and salt and pepper to taste
and pour over the olives.
4 Brush the egg slices and tomatoes with
mayonnaise.
5 Serve with shredded Chinese leaves and tiny new
potatoes with a pat of parsley butter.

Salade Toutes Saisons

Lettuce hearts require less washing because they are tight and firm.
Do not substitute fresh for evaporated milk or the sauce will curdle.

2 round lettuce hearts
½ cucumber
1 very small bulb fennel
2 small oranges
1 oz/30g shelled hazelnuts and
almonds, mixed
3 tablespoons unsweetened
evaporated milk
Sea salt
Freshly ground black pepper

1 Wash the lettuce and separate the leaves. Spin or
shake in a clean teacloth.
2 Slice the cucumber. Trim and finely slice the
fennel.
3 Grate the zest from both oranges. Squeeze the juice
from 1 orange, remove the pith and slice the
remaining orange. Coarsely chop the nuts.
4 Chill the milk in the freezer for 15 minutes, then
beat with a whisk until thick. Stir in the orange juice
and grated zest and season with salt and pepper.
5 Pour into a wooden salad bowl. Add the salad and
ingredients and toss with the dressing. Garnish with
the orange slices.
6 Serve with potato salad and a grated carrot salad.

Shelly's Salad _____

Any small pasta shapes can be substituted although the shells are especially attractive.

6 oz/170g wholemeal pasta shells
5 tablespoons natural yogurt
4 tablespoons mango chutney
8 tablespoons mayonnaise (see pages 29 or 37)
1 small red pepper
6 oz/170g tiny button mushrooms
2 large bananas
1 box alfalfa

1 Cook the pasta according to the directions on the packet. Meanwhile mix the yogurt, mango chutney and mayonnaise in a large bowl.
2 Core, de-seed and dice the red pepper and add to the bowl with the mushrooms.
3 Halve the bananas lengthwise, remove the flesh and slice finely. Fold into the mixture with the drained warm pasta.
4 Spoon the salad on to individual plates and garnish with a banana shell filled with alfalfa.

Simply Corn on the Cob _____

The oven method of cooking corn cobs takes longer than when boiled in a saucepan, but they do not have to be watched so carefully which could rob you of vital time in the preparation of other dishes.

Salad oil
4-6 fresh large corn cobs
2 oz/55g butter
Sea salt
Freshly ground black pepper
5 tablespoons mayonnaise (see pages 29 or 37)
1 tablespoon freshly chopped parsley
6 tablespoons low-fat natural yogurt
1 tablespoon chopped chives

1 Roughly tear foil squares large enough to wrap around the individual cobs. Wipe inside the foil squares with a crumpled piece of kitchen paper moistened with oil.
2 Wrap each cob tightly in foil, twisting the end Christmas cracker fashion.
3 Place the packets in a hot oven 400°F/200°C/Gas Mark 6 for 25-35 minutes.
4 Meanwhile prepare three small serving bowls of dressing. In one place the butter, season with salt and pepper; mix the mayonnaise and parsley in the second; and combine the yogurt with salt, pepper and chives in the third.
5 Remove the foil packets from the oven. Switch off the heat and put the bowl containing the butter in the still hot oven to melt.
6 Pile the unopened packets on to a serving dish and

put corn holders or wooden cocktail sticks in a glass
on the table and place the bowls of dressing at the
side of the dish.

Smokey Spinach Salad

About 8 oz/225g fresh spinach
8 oz/225g smoked tofu
4 thin slices wholemeal bread
Oil for frying
2 cloves garlic, crushed
1 teaspoon sesame seed oil
1 level teaspoon sesame seeds
1 tablespoon white wine
vinegar
Sea salt
Freshly ground black pepper

1 Wash the spinach and remove the coarse stalks.
Pat the leaves dry and layer on a chopping board and
shred with a stainless steel knife.
2 Drain the tofu, press with kitchen towel paper to
dry and cut into small cubes. Remove the crusts and
dice the bread. Cut the tofu into cubes.
3 Pour about 1 inch/2.5cm oil into a large frying-
pan. Stir in the garlic and heat until hazy, then fry
the croûtons, tossing frequently until golden
4 Remove the croûtons with a slotted spoon and
drain on kitchen paper.
5 Making sure the oil is hot, fry the tofu. Drain
thoroughly.
6 Put the sesame oil and seeds in a small saucepan,
put on the lid and cook for 2 minutes, shaking the
pan all the time. Remove from the heat and leave to
cool down, then stir in the vinegar. Season with salt
and pepper.
7 Pour into a wooden salad bowl. Add the spinach,
tofu and croûtons, toss well and serve at once.

Spinach and Mushroom Compôte

QC Serves 4
Takes about 30 minutes

This last minute main course requires only the purchase of soured cream but UHT or tinned cream and a little lemon juice can be substituted.

1 lb/455g frozen chopped spinach
5 oz/140g tin tomato purée
½ pint/285ml soured cream
1×8 oz/225g tin mushrooms
½ teaspoon dried marjoram
Sea salt
Freshly ground black pepper
2 tablespoons grated Parmesan

1 Drain the spinach thoroughly, then mix with the tomato purée, cream, drained mushrooms and marjoram together with a little salt and pepper.
2 Spoon into a greased 6 inch/15cm soufflé dish. Sprinkle with the Parmesan. Bake in a moderate oven 350°F/180°C/Gas Mark 4 for 20-30 minutes.
3 Serve with duchesse potatoes.

Opposite *Okra and Tomato Hotpot (page 109).*

*Surprise Jimboes with Beetroot Relish*___PA Serves 4

This recipe is a huge success — it consists of a deep-fried split peas casing around a cherry tomato, the whole served with the beetroot relish.

1 medium cooked beetroot
¼ cucumber
¼ pint/140ml soured cream
Sea salt
Freshly ground black pepper
½ teaspoon ground cumin
¼ teaspoon ground ginger
1 medium onion
1 oz/30g butter
12 oz/340g yellow split peas
½ teaspoon bay leaf powder
Sea salt
2 eggs, beaten
8 cherry tomatoes or pearl onions

Optional Advance Preparations

Up to 2 days ahead

1 Peel and grate the beetroot and cucumber. Season the cream with salt and pepper and stir in the cumin and ginger. Mix with the beetroot and cucumber. Set aside.

2 Peel and chop the onion and fry in the butter until soft. Stir in the split peas and add 1¾ pints/1 litre water, the bay leaf powder and some black pepper.

3 Bring to the boil, then simmer for about 1 hour, stirring frequently as the mixture thickens to prevent sticking. When soft beat the peas until smooth and season with salt and pepper. Leave to cool, then mix in the beaten eggs.

To assemble

4 Divide the mixture into eight and using floured hands mould each around a tomato or pearl onion to form eight balls, each completely enclosed in the mashed split peas.

5 Pour 2 inches/5cm oil into a deep saucepan. Heat the oil and fry the balls a few at a time, turning them over as soon as they are immersed to maintain an even shape. When cut through the tomatoes should remain whole and almost raw.

6 Drain on kitchen paper and serve with the beetroot relish.

Opposite *Apricot and Raisin Mousse (page 141); Pink Yogurt (page 152); and Peach Daiquiri (page 150).*

Swiss Asparagus Roulade _____PA ★ Serves 4-5

Use either the very thin young asparagus which is plentiful in mid-summer or frozen asparagus spears which are 'meatier' than tinned asparagus.

1½ oz/40g butter
1¼ oz/35g plain flour
½ pint/285ml milk
7 oz/200g grated Gruyère cheese
Sea salt
Freshly ground black pepper
2 oz/55g wholemeal breadcrumbs
4 eggs, separated
¼ pint/140ml single cream
4 tablespoons grated Parmesan
12 oz/340g asparagus tips

Optional Advance Preparations

Up to 24 hours ahead for refrigerator storage or 2 weeks ahead for freezer storage (the sauce should be removed from the freezer 24 hours ahead)

1 Prepare a thick sauce. Melt the butter in a saucepan, then stir in the flour. Gradually add the milk and cook, stirring all the time until boiling and thickened.

2 Continue cooking for a further minute. Stir in 1 oz/30g of the Gruyère. Season with salt and pepper. Cover with a dampened disc of greaseproof paper, cool and store.

Up to 24 hours ahead

3 Mix the remaining Gruyère with the breadcrumbs and egg yolks and beat in the cream. Season with salt and pepper. Cover and refrigerate on the top shelf.

40 minutes before serving

4 Prepare a moderately hot oven 400°F/200°C/Gas Mark 6. Grease and line the base and sides of a 12×8 inch/30×22cm Swiss roll tin with non-stick baking parchment.

5 Beat the egg whites stiffly. Stir 1 tablespoon of the beaten whites into the breadcrumbs and egg yolk sauce, then fold in the remainder.

6 Pour into the prepared tin, tipping the tin to spread the mixture evenly. Avoid using a knife which tends to knock out the air. Sprinkle with half the Parmesan. Bake in the centre of the oven for 15 minutes or until just firm.

7 While the roulade is baking cook the asparagus in salted water. Drain and remove any tough stems.

8 Reheat the sauce, beating vigorously to remove any

lumps and add a little milk or asparagus liquor if necessary.

9 Turn the baked base out on to another sheet of non-stick baking parchment and lightly sprinkle with the remaining Parmesan.

To assemble

10 Spread the sauce evenly over the roulade base and arrange the cooked asparagus across the width, making sure that some tips are showing at either edge. Using the paper as a guide, roll up Swiss roll fashion, starting at one short end.

11 Serve at once from a hot dish with a green side salad.

Tomates Gratinées

QC ★ Serves 4
Takes about 35 minutes

Omit the pasta and you can serve the tomatoes as a quick cook starter on a disc of wholemeal toast.

8 firm medium tomatoes
1 tablespoon sunflower oil
Sea salt
Freshly ground black pepper
3 tablespoons fresh wholemeal breadcrumbs
2 tablespoons grated cheese
1 small onion
1 tablespoon scissored basil leaves
8 oz/225g fresh wholemeal pasta shells
½ oz/15g butter

1 Halve the tomatoes and place in a greased oven-to-table dish, brush with oil and sprinkle with salt and pepper.

2 Mix the breadcrumbs, cheese, finely chopped onion and basil together and pile on the tomatoes.

3 Bake in a moderate oven 350°F/180°C/Gas Mark 4 for 25 minutes until cooked and brown.

4 Meanwhile cook the pasta in boiling salted water. When the tomatoes are ready drain the pasta, toss with butter and spoon around the tomatoes.

5 Serve with cucumber and onion salad mixed with a little yogurt.

Vegetable Gratin _____PA Serves 3-4

A mixture of mainly root vegetables baked in a creamy sauce and
garnished with browned almonds.

8 oz/225g potatoes
8 oz/225g carrots
½ head celery
8 oz/225g salsify
4 oz/115g tiny onions
Sea salt
2 oz/55g butter
1 oz/30g wholemeal flour
½ pint/285ml milk
4 tablespoons chopped parsley
2 tablespoons grated Edam
cheese
¼ pint/140ml single cream
2 tablespoons toasted flaked
almonds

Optional Advance Preparations

Up to 24 hours ahead

1 Peel and dice the potatoes. Scrape and slice the
carrots. Slice the celery. Scrape and slice the salsify.
Peel the onions.
2 Boil the vegetables together in salted water for 5
minutes to blanch. Drain and cool. Turn into a deep
well-greased flameproof dish.

Up to 12 hours ahead

3 Put the butter, flour and milk in a thick-based
saucepan and add the parsley. Gradually bring to the
boil, stirring continuously until the sauce thickens.
4 Stir in the cheese. Cover the surface with a disc of
dampened greaseproof paper. Set aside.

To assemble (up to 1 hour ahead)

5 Beat the cream into the sauce and season with salt
and pepper. Pour over the vegetables.
6 Put into the centre of the oven and bake at
350°F/180°C/Gas Mark 4 for 15 minutes or until hot.
Sprinkle with the browned almonds. Serve hot.

*Vegetable Kebab Salad*_____PA ★ Serves 4-6

Preparing the vegetables and frying the bread will take about 40
minutes. Allow about 30 minutes for threading on to the skewers.

¼ pint/140ml French dressing
2 tablespoons freshly chopped
parsley
1 tablespoon finely scissored
basil leaves
1 teaspoon double cream
1 small cauliflower
1 small green pepper
1 small red pepper
½ cucumber
12 baby tomatoes
12 tiny new potatoes
12 button mushrooms
12 bottled pearl onions
2 slices wholemeal bread
1 garlic clove
Sunflower oil
12 stuffed green olives
1 lettuce

Optional Advance Preparations

12-24 hours ahead

1 Divide the French dressing between three bowls,
adding the parsley to one, the basil to the second and
the cream to the third.

2 Prepare the vegetables: separate the cauliflower
florets, core, seed and dice the peppers and cut into
1 inch/2.5cm pieces. Cut the cucumber into thick
chunks. Peel and pierce the tomatoes once or twice.
Boil the potatoes until tender but not too soft.

3 Divide the vegetables, including the mushrooms
and pearl onions but not the olives and garlic,
between the three bowls.

4 Cover and refrigerate, stirring when you can to
ensure that the vegetables are all coated.

5 Cut the bread into 1 inch/2.5cm squares. Crush
the garlic. Pour about 1 inch/2.5cm oil into a frying-
pan. Heat the oil and add the garlic.

6 Fry the bread squares on both sides until golden. If
the oil is hot enough the croûtons will cook in 20
seconds. Drain on kitchen paper. Store in an airtight
container in the refrigerator.

2-3 hours ahead

7 Thread 12 small flat-sided skewers with a mixed
selection of the vegetables from the first bowl and the
bread squares. Thread the vegetables from the second
and third bowls similarly. Include the olives with the
vegetables from the third bowl.

To assemble

8 Arrange the skewers on a bed of shredded lettuce
on a large platter and refrigerate until required.

Vegetable Pilau Rice _____PA Serves 8

Basmati rice is sold in most supermarkets in 1 lb/455g packs. Use
this recipe as a complete main course or omit the vegetables and
serve with curries, patties or cutlets.

About 8 oz/225g prepared
vegetables including
cauliflower, beans, swedes,
carrots and onions
1 lb/455g Basmati rice
4 tablespoons sunflower oil
6 whole cardamoms
4 cloves
6 black peppercorns
2 bay leaves
½ teaspoon turmeric
1 oz/30g cashew nuts
1 oz/30g pine nuts
1 oz/30g raisins

Optional Advance Preparations

Up to 2 months ahead

1 Cook the vegetables in salted water. Drain,
reserving the liquor and finely chop the vegetables.
2 Put the rice in a large strainer, lower into a mixing
bowl of cold water and stir the rice so that all the
grains have a chance to float. Drain, change the water
and repeat at least six times until the water runs clear.
Drain, then soak in about 2 pints/1.1 litres cold water
for half an hour. Strain and leave to dry.
3 Heat the oil in a heavy-based saucepan or cast iron
casserole dish. When the oil is hot add the
cardamoms, cloves, peppercorns and bay leaves. Fry
for 1 minute until the spices begin to pop.
4 Add the turmeric, then the rice and fry briskly,
stirring constantly with a wooden spoon for one
minute as the mixture is inclined to stick.
5 Make up the reserved cooking liquor to 1 pint/
570ml with water and add to the pan. Add the
vegetables. Stir well, bring to the boil, then reduce the
heat to minimum. Cover with a lid and overwrap the
lid with foil to form a tight seal.
6 Cook for 25 minutes, then remove the pan from
the heat. Leave to stand for 5 minutes, then gently
fork up the rice. When cool, freeze into required
portions.

To assemble

7 Thaw the vegetable rice at room temperature.
Reheat in the microwave or in a colander over a pan
of simmering water.
8 Add the nuts and raisins and serve hot.

Wholefoodie Salad _____PA Serves 4-6

A crunchy, fruity salad for all.

4 tablespoons whole green lentils
6 oz/170g roast buckwheat
Oil for cooking
2 medium carrots
1 small red pepper
2 oz/55g sultanas
2 tablespoons red wine vinegar
6 tablespoons sunflower oil
Sea salt
Freshly ground black pepper
1 dessert apple

Optional Advance Preparations

About 6 days ahead

1 Prepare the lentils for sprouting. Put them in a large jar. Cover with water and leave in a refrigerator for 24 hours.
2 Rinse the lentils and change the water, repeating every 12 hours or so. No real changes occur for the first three days but thereafter the shoots begin to appear.

Up to 3 days ahead

3 Cook the buckwheat. Put the oil in a saucepan and when hot add the buckwheat and cook for 5 minutes to bring out the roasted flavour.
4 Add 1¾ pints/1 litre boiling water and simmer for about 15 minutes until the buckwheat is tender but not soft. Drain, cover and leave to cool. Refrigerate.

Up to 6 hours ahead

5 Peel and grate the carrots. Core, seed and dice the red pepper. Mix with the buckwheat, sultanas, vinegar and oil and season with salt and pepper.
6 Peel, core and slice the apple. Fold into the salad and refrigerate.

To assemble

7 Drain, rinse and drain the sprouted lentils again. Spread over the salad.

Wild Rice Salad

QC ★ Serves 4
Takes about 40 minutes

Wild rice is not really related to the rice family as it is a grass.
However it is similar in shape, lighter in texture and is very dark in
colour. Wild rice is very expensive and in the luxury class. You
could mix it with long-grain white rice if you wish.

3 celery sticks
1 bunch spring onions
4 oz/115g wild rice
6 oz/170g frozen or cooked peas
2 vegetable stock cubes
½ teaspoon yeast extract
1 round lettuce
About 2 oz/55g Brazil nuts

Dressing

2 tablespoons safflower oil
1 tablespoon shoyu sauce
½ teaspoon raw cane sugar
½ tablespoon cider vinegar

1 Finely slice the celery. Trim and slice the spring onions.
2 Cook the wild rice according to the packet instructions, adding the peas and celery, stock cubes and yeast extract.
3 While the rice is cooking, wash the whole lettuce in several changes of cold water and place upside-down to drain. Remove and discard the coarse stalk end. Twist out the heart, then shred it finely.
4 Mix in the spring onions. Put the outer leaves, still connected to the stalk, in a deep wooden salad bowl.
5 Put the Brazil nuts into a small pan, cover with cold water and bring to the boil. Drain and slice the nuts.
6 Beat all the dressing ingredients together. Mix into the rice. Fill the lettuce with layers of rice mixture and shredded lettuce and sprinkle with the sliced nuts.
7 Serve at room temperature with chunky wholemeal bread and a tomato salad.

Yorkshire Coracles

Surprisingly filling little 'buns' with a vegetable purée centre,
topped with millet flakes.

Batter
5 oz/140g wholemeal flour
Pinch sea salt
2 eggs
½ pint/285ml milk
Oil for patty tins

Filling
1 oz/30g millet flakes
1 oz/30g butter
1 oz/30g white flour
¼ pint/140ml milk
*8 oz/225g frozen spinach
pellets or chopped fresh
spinach*
1 tablespoon chopped chives
2 oz/55g frozen peas
Sea salt
Freshly ground black pepper

1 Sift the flour into a large bowl. Reserve the bran.
Add the salt, eggs and milk and beat until smooth.
Leave to stand for 10-15 minutes.

2 Meanwhile heat the oven to 425°F/220°C/Gas
Mark 7.

3 Place a teaspoon of oil in each of sixteen individual
bun tins and heat in the oven until the oil begins to
smoke.

4 One-third fill each tin with batter and bake at the
top of the oven for about 15 minutes or until the
puddings are risen and golden.

5 While the batter is standing toast the millet flakes.

6 While the batter is baking, melt the butter and stir
in the flour. Cook over a moderate heat for 1 minute.

7 Remove the pan from the heat and beat in the
milk. Add the spinach and half the reserved bran.
The remainder can be returned to the packet.

8 Cook, stirring continuously, until the sauce begins
to thicken. Stir in the chives and peas, season with
salt and pepper and cook for a further 4 minutes.

9 Serve the coracles as soon as they are baked and
well risen, filled with the pea and spinach purée and
topped with a sprinkling of toasted millet flakes.

10 Serve with cooked carrots.

Young Mushroom Salad

In this predominantly mushroom salad the tiny variety should be
used for greatest effect. Tinned baby mushrooms or quartered
button mushrooms can be used instead. Although the sauce can be
prepared without a blender, there is a greater chance of curdling.

*1 lb/455g tiny button
mushrooms
1 bunch watercress
1 bunch spring onions
1 tablespoon pine nuts
1 garlic clove
1 egg
1 tablespoon ground almonds
1 tablespoon fresh lemon juice
2 tablespoons hazelnut oil
2 tablespoons sunflower oil
Sea salt
Freshly ground black pepper
Dill weed*

1 Wipe the mushrooms. Wash, dry and trim the
thicker stalks from the watercress. Tear the cress into
small sprigs. Trim and finely slice the spring onions.
Mix together in a large bowl.

2 Make a sauce using the liquidizer or food
processor. Switch on at full speed and pour the pine
nuts and the garlic through the aperture.

3 As soon as the nuts are finely chopped and with
the motor still running, add the egg and ground
almonds. When the mixture lightens, switch off and
scrape down the sides of the goblet or bowl. Add the
lemon juice.

4 Switch on again and pour in the oils in a steady
trickle. When the sauce thickens, season with salt and
pepper. Spoon over the vegetables and stir gently
until they are well covered.

5 Transfer to a wooden salad bowl and garnish with
dill weed.

6 Serve with a side plate of sliced tomato sprinkled
with dill weed.

6 Desserts

The busy cook can hardly be expected to produce 'the trolley' when dessert time comes round. Having worked all day and probably been up late the night before to say nothing of the nervous energy used during the run-up to that ring on the door bell, at this point in the proceedings the host is fairly if not completely exhausted.

However there should be sufficient variety in this short chapter to be able to provide more than one choice. Either pick out one hot and one cold recipe or two cold desserts, but do not try to offer two last-minute cooked dishes — for example Crêpes Suzette and Caribbean Bananas.

Purchase cream on the day or before the 'expiry date' or keep a few boxes of UHT cream in the larder or frozen cream in the freezer. Even in these cholesterol-conscious times there will be plenty of takers. Single cream has the lowest calorie count and a minimum fat content of 18%, whipping cream has 35% fat and double cream 48% fat. Allow ¼ pint/140ml for four to five people.

*Apple and Fig Flan*_____PA Serves 4-6

If the pastry case is baked in a loose-bottomed flan tin, the flan can
be unmoulded before filling. Alternatively use a fluted flan dish if
you can spare it during storage of the flan.

*3 oz/85g 100% wholemeal
plain flour
3 oz/85g plain white flour
3 oz/85g soft margarine
3-4 tablespoons cold milk
7 oz/200g Quark
3 oz/85g icing sugar
2 red apples
4 fresh figs
½ pint/285ml pure apple
juice
1 tablespoon honey
2 teaspoons agar agar or
Gelazone*

Optional Advance Preparations

Up to 2 weeks ahead

1 Sift the flours together, replacing any bran left in
the sieve. Rub in the margarine, add sufficient milk to
form a soft dough.
2 Chill for half an hour, then roll out on a floured
surface to fit a greased 8 inch/20cm flan dish. Press a
piece of greased foil on to the pastry and bake in a
hot oven 400°F/200°C/Gas Mark 6 for 15 minutes.
Remove the foil and bake for a further 5-10 minutes.
Leave to cool, then overwrap with freezer foil and
store in a cool place.

To assemble

3 Blend the Quark and icing sugar together. Spread
over the base of the flan case.
4 Remove the stalks and cut the figs into quarters.
Quarter, core and thinly slice the apples and arrange
in overlapping slices in the pastry case, showing the
red skin. Arrange the figs in a 'spoke' design on top.
5 Mix the apple juice, honey and agar agar in a
saucepan and heat gently, whisking frequently.
Remove from the heat. Immediately pour the sauce
evenly over the figs and refrigerate until set.
6 Serve with cream if you wish.

Apricot and Raisin Mousse
NC   Serves 4
Takes about 10 minutes plus chilling

This is a textured rather than a smooth mousse, relying on the fruit
for its sweetness.

1 large egg
14 oz/400g fromage frais
2 tablespoons double cream
1 tablespoon apricot brandy
5 oz/140g ready-to-eat dried
apricots
3 oz/85g raisins
Raw cane granulated sugar
4 lemon slices for decoration

1 Separate the egg and beat the yolk with the cheese, cream and apricot brandy until smooth.

2 Very finely chop or mix the apricots and fold into the mixture. Stir in the raisins.

3 Using clean beaters whisk the egg white until stiff. Brush the rims of four glass goblets with a little of the egg white and dip them in the sugar.

4 Fold the remaining egg white into the fruit mixture and carefully pour into the goblets.

5 Refrigerate overnight if possible or chill in the freezer for 15 minutes before serving.

6 Decorate each glass with a lemon slice, slit to the centre and hooked over the rim.

Bananes au Citron
QC   Serves 4
Takes about 10 minutes

A simple recipe which will look very attractive served on small
brightly-coloured plates.

2 oz/55g raw cane sugar
5 tablespoons water
1 lemon
1 lb/455g bananas
2 tablespoons chopped
pistachios, to decorate

1 Stir the sugar and water together in a small saucepan and heat slowly until the sugar has dissolved.

2 Raise the heat and, without stirring, cook until boiling, then continue cooking for 2 minutes until a thin syrup is formed.

3 Squeeze the lemon juice on to a plate. Peel the bananas, slice thinly and dip into the lemon juice.

4 Arrange in overlapping rings on individual plates and pour the syrup over. Sprinkle with chopped pistachios.

Caribbean Bananas

QC Serves 4
Takes about 15 minutes

Before embarking on this recipe make sure that the bananas will fit
into the frying-pan being used.

1½ oz/40g raw cane sugar
¼ teaspoon vanilla essence
5 tablespoons water
8 small bananas
1½ oz/40g dark dessert
chocolate
3 tablespoons dark rum

1 Combine the sugar, vanilla essence and water in a
frying-pan and heat gently, stirring continuously,
until the sugar has dissolved. Raise the heat and cook
until boiling, then fast boil for a further minute.
2 Peel the bananas, put into the syrup and cook for
3 minutes, basting frequently. Remove with a slotted
spoon and put on a heated flameproof serving dish.
3 Break up the chocolate and stir into the syrup
until it has melted, then pour over the bananas.
4 Warm the rum in a metal tablespoon over a flame
or in a small saucepan for 30 seconds. Pour over the
bananas and immediately ignite. Serve at once with
whipped cream if wished.

Crêpes Suzette

PA Serves 4-5

The busy cook can prepare this luxury dessert which is normally
time-consuming. Use a 6 inch/15cm frying-pan to achieve well-
shaped crêpes. There is sufficient batter in this recipe to allow for
two or three per person.

Batter

3 oz/85g plain white flour
3 oz/85g wholemeal flour
¼ teaspoon sea salt
2 eggs
¾ pint/425ml milk
1 teaspoon sunflower oil
Butter or oil for greasing the
pan

Optional Advance Preparations

*Up to 24 hours ahead if stored in the refrigerator or
1 month ahead if stored in the freezer*

1 To make the pancakes, mix the flours and salt in a
bowl. Make a well in the centre and pour in the eggs,
milk and oil.
2 Using a wooden spoon, stir the liquid, gradually
drawing in the flour until the batter is smooth. The
batter should be the consistency of single cream and
will thicken upon standing.
3 Heat a small frying-pan with just enough oil or
butter to grease the base. When hot pour 1
tablespoon of the batter on to the centre of the pan

Sauce
2 *oranges*
3 *oz/85g unsalted butter*
2 *oz/55g soft dark brown*
sugar
4 *tablespoons* Grand Marnier
or Cointreau
1 *tablespoon brandy*

and tilt the handle to spread the batter evenly. If the batter does not run freely, it is too thick and you must stir more milk into the remaining mixture before cooking the next crêpe.

4 Leave to set, shake the pan to loosen the crêpe, then flip it over with a palette knife and cook for about 15 seconds.

5 Cook the remaining crêpes and stack between sheets of greaseproof paper if you intend to store them in the refrigerator or between cling film or non-stick baking parchment for freezer storage. When the crêpes are cool overwrap with foil and store.

Up to 24 hours ahead

6 Grate the orange zest, squeeze the juice and put both in a large frying-pan with the butter and sugar. Cook over moderate heat, stirring until the sugar has dissolved, then bring to the boil. Stir in the *Grand Marnier* or *Cointreau*. Cover and leave to cool.

About 1 hour before serving

7 Take out and unwrap the crêpes and leave at room temperature.

To assemble

8 Heat the syrup until boiling and add the crêpes one at a time, folding each in half and then in half again in the pan. Push towards the side of the pan to make space for the next one.

9 When all the crêpes are heated, transfer to a heated serving dish. Bring the syrup remaining in the pan to the boil. Add the brandy, set alight and pour over the crêpes. Serve at once.

Crunchy Fruit Salad _____NC Serves 4

Fruit salad is simple to prepare but you must allow plenty of time.
Prepare the pears, apples and bananas last to avoid discoloration.

2 pieces candied orange peel
4 fresh dates
About 2 oz/55g hazelnuts
6 or 7 digestive wheatmeal biscuits
1 large orange
1 red-skinned apple
1 green dessert apple
1 firm pear
1 large firm banana
6 tablespoons natural yogurt

1 Cut one piece of candied peel into strips and reserve for decoration. Finely chop the other. Stone and finely chop the dates and the hazelnuts.
2 Put the biscuits in a polythene bag and crush with a rolling pin or empty bottle.
3 Grate and reserve the orange rind. Peel the orange on a wooden board vertically with a sharp knife to reveal the flesh. Segment over the salad bowl to catch any escaping juices.
4 Rinse, quarter, core and slice the apples and the pear and after mixing with the orange, slice and add the banana.
5 Add the chopped peel, dates and hazelnuts and stir in the yogurt. Sprinkle with the biscuit crumbs and grated rind. Decorate with the candied peel strips arranged as spokes.

Edwardian Blackcurrant Pudding _____QC Serves 4-6
Takes about 30 minutes

A cheap-to-make pudding when blackcurrants are in season, but
out of season frozen blackcurrants are excellent. Thaw them in the
pie dish before baking.

1 lb/455g blackcurrants
2 tablespoons clear honey
½ teaspoon mixed spice
3 oz/85g finely grated wholemeal breadcrumbs
4 oz/115g soft dark brown sugar
1 oz/30g vegetable shredded suet

1 Preheat the oven to 400°F/200°C/Gas Mark 6.
2 Remove the stalks and wash the blackcurrants. Put into a greased 2 pint/1.1 litre flameproof dish. Mix in the honey and spice.
3 Mix the breadcrumbs, sugar and suet together. Spread over the fruit.
4 Put the dish on a baking tray and bake in the hot oven for 20 minutes or until the topping is deep brown. Serve with natural yogurt.

Fresh Fruit Salad

When calculating quantities allow about 1½ fruits or portions of
fruit per person. Include some citrus fruit to maintain a good colour
but do not use soft red fruits which would tint all the paler fruits.
You can only use fruit in season so you may have to vary those in
my list. It is not worth making fruit salad for smaller numbers
which would limit the selection of fruit.

1 lemon
2–4 tablespoons demerara
sugar
1 orange
1 green dessert apple
1 banana
4 oz/115g bunch black grapes
1 fresh peach
4 oz/115g red cherries
2 kiwi fruit

1 Grate the rind and squeeze the lemon juice into a
decorative bowl. Stir in the sugar.
2 Peel the orange and remove the segments over the
bowl to save the juices.
3 Add the quartered, cored and diced apple and the
peeled and sliced banana. Halve the grapes and
remove the pips. Rinse the peach, remove the stone
and slice the flesh. Stone the cherries if possible.
4 Mix all this fruit with the sweetened citrus juices
and toss with clean hands (if you do this with spoons
the fruit may become damaged).
5 Slice the kiwi fruit, then peel away the skin.
Arrange in overlapping circles around the sides of the
bowl.

Grand Marnier Mousse en Boîte _____PA Serves 4-6

This is a rich dessert full of sugar, cream and egg yolks that health experts may frown upon, but it is nice to have a splurge occasionally.

Meringue

3 egg whites
6 oz/170g caster sugar

Mousse

3 egg yolks
3 oz/85g caster sugar
½ pint/285ml double cream
2 tablespoons Grand Marnier
Grated zest of 1 orange
Fresh orange segments, to decorate

Optional Advance Preparations

Up to 1 month ahead

1 Make the meringue case. Separate the eggs and beat the whites with grease-free beaters until stiff peaks form. Gradually whisk in half the sugar, a teaspoon at a time. Fold in the remaining sugar with a tablespoon. Spoon into a piping bag fitted with a ½ inch/1cm nozzle.

2 Pencil a 6 inch/15cm circle on a sheet of non-stick baking parchment. Reverse on to a baking tray. Pipe the meringue in a flat spiral to cover the circle completely.

3 Place in a slow oven, 300°F/150°C/Gas Mark 2 for 10 minutes to set the meringue slightly.

4 Remove from the oven, and pipe a border of meringue over the circumference. Bake for 5 minutes, then repeat the process to build up a wall. Bake for about 1½ hours until the meringue is firm and crisp on the outside. The colour should not be pure white.

5 Reverse on to the baking tray and bake for a further 10 minutes. Leave to cool, then store in an airtight container.

6 Prepare the mousse. Beat the egg yolks and strain into a mixing bowl. Add the sugar and beat with an electric whisk until very thick when a spoonful of the mixture will rest on the surface without sinking.

7 In another bowl beat the cream and *Grand Marnier* together until softly whipped. Grate in the orange rind. Fold the cream and orange rind into the mousse.

8 Shape double thickness foil into a dish shape which would fit inside the meringue case. Turn the mousse into this dish and open freeze for two hours. Overwrap and freeze until required.

To assemble

9 About one hour before serving, unmould the mousse into the meringue case. Decorate with well drained fresh orange segments. Chill until ready to serve.

Iced Coffee Mousse

NC   Serves 4
Takes about 15 minutes plus chilling

This mousse may be served chilled. If it has been frozen allow 30 minutes at room temperature to thaw.

1 large egg
1 lb/455g fromage blanc
3 oz/85g raw cane sugar
About 2 teaspoons coffee extract
Sugar coffee beans, for decoration

1 Separate the egg. Beat the yolk with the cheese and the sugar until the mixture is thick and mousse-like. Stir in the coffee essence.
2 Beat the egg white to stiff peaks using clean beaters. Fold thoroughly into the mousse.
3 Pour into four individual ramekins and chill for 30-45 minutes until firm but not frozen.
4 Serve with sponge finger biscuits and decorate with sugar coffee beans.

Jubilee Cherries

QC   Serves 4
Takes about 10 minutes

Unfortunately pitted or stoned cherries are not always easy to obtain. If you are using the unpitted variety it is advisable to warn your guests.

2 oz/55g block vanilla ice cream
14½ oz/410g tin black pitted cherries
1 tablespoon arrowroot
3 tablespoons brandy

1 First put the ice cream on to individual plates and refrigerate.
2 Drain the cherries carefully into a measuring jug and make up the juice to 8 fl oz/225ml with cold water.
3 Blend in the arrowroot. Pour into a saucepan and bring to the boil over gentle heat, stirring all the time until the sauce is thick. Add the cherries and cook until hot — the sauce will thin slightly.
4 Put the brandy into a small pan and heat for 15-20 seconds. Quickly pour over the cherries and ignite immediately. You *can* heat the brandy in an undecorated cup in the microwave, but do not ignite in the cup. Wait until the brandy touches the cherries.

Malakoff Torte _____PA Serves 8-12

This is a very rich cake. Undecorated it will keep for several weeks
in a freezer but should not be kept too long in a warm atmosphere.

*3 oz/85g plain dessert
chocolate
6 oz/170g butter
6 oz/170g soft light brown
sugar
1 egg yolk
1 tablespoon sherry or rum
About 1½ packets sponge
fingers
Glacé cherries, to decorate*

Optional Advance Preparations

Up to 1 month ahead

1 Line a 1 lb/455g loaf tin with greaseproof paper.
2 Break up the chocolate and put into a glass bowl
over a pan of very hot water until melted or melt in
the microwave oven.
3 While the bowl is still over the saucepan add the
butter and sugar and stir until the sugar has
dissolved. Beat, then strain in the egg yolk and mix
thoroughly. Remove from the heat.
4 Put the sherry or rum on a plate and quickly dip
in the sponge fingers. Place the biscuits in the base of
the tin, fitting in the broken pieces where necessary.
Cover with a layer of the chocolate sauce.
5 Continue alternating layers of biscuits and sauce,
finishing with the sauce. Cover with greaseproof
paper and put a weight on top to prevent the biscuits
from floating. Freeze or if to be used within 24 hours
refrigerate.

To assemble

6 Turn the torte out on to a serving plate lined with
a paper doily and decorate the top with glacé cherries.

Marmalade Roll _____PA Serves 6

This pastry is made with a mixture of wholemeal and plain white
flours which I find delicious. You could use entirely 81 per cent
extraction flour if you wish but it is more difficult to roll out.

6 oz/170g 100% wholemeal plain flour
6 oz/170g plain white flour
Pinch sea salt
5 oz/140g soft margarine
3-4 tablespoons cold milk
About ½ jar thick-cut marmalade
Beaten egg or milk to glaze

Optional Advance Preparations

Up to 1 month ahead

1 Sift the flours and salt together and set the bran aside. Add the margarine and mix in with two round-bladed knives. Add sufficient milk to bind. Gather into a ball and wrap in cling film. Refrigerate for 1 hour.

2 Roll out the pastry on baking parchment to a rectangle about 11×8 inches/27×20cm and sprinkle with the reserved bran.

3 Brush a 1 inch/2.5cm border of the pastry with beaten egg. Spread the marmalade along one long side of the pastry to within 1 inch/2.5cm of the three edges.

4 Roll up from the long edge and you will find that the marmalade will spread itself out as you go.

5 Leave a border of about 1½ inches/4cm at the other long edge of the pastry without covering it with marmalade and seal this edge against the roll.

6 Carefully lift the roll still on the baking parchment on to a baking tray. Press the pastry ends to seal and trim away any jagged edges. Brush the pastry with beaten egg or milk.

7 Open freeze until firm, then roll up in baking parchment around the pastry. Remove from the baking tray, cover and freeze.

To assemble

8 Remove the marmalade roll from the freezer about two hours ahead of serving.

9 About one hour ahead of serving heat a fairly hot oven 400°F/200°C/Gas Mark 6. Place the wrapped roll on a baking tray, open out the parchment and smooth against the tray.

10 Bake the roll for 20 minutes, then reduce the temperature to 375°F/190°C/Gas Mark 5 and bake for about 15 further minutes until the pastry is golden.

11 Leave for a few minutes before serving as the marmalade becomes very hot inside the pastry.

Orange Brulette

Some guests may dislike yogurt. If you have one of these you could
substitute half whipped double cream.

1 oz/30g dates
1 orange
1 pear
¼ pint/140ml full cream
natural yogurt
2 teaspoons clear honey
2 oz/55g butter
2 oz/55g demerara sugar
2 oz/55g porridge oats

1 Chop the dates. Peel, segment and chop the
orange. Peel, core and dice the pear.
2 Blend the yogurt and honey and mix with the
fruit. Divide between four or six individual ramekins.
Chill in the freezer for 10 minutes.
3 Meanwhile melt the butter in a saucepan. Stir in
the sugar and cook over moderate heat, stirring
continuously until the sugar dissolves. Mix in the
oats.
4 Switch on the grill. Spoon the topping over the
fruit but do not press it down. Put the dishes into the
grill pan with six or seven ice cubes and grill until the
topping is brown.

Peach Daiquiri

A daiquiri is a thick cocktail which is delicious when served chilled
as a light dessert. Garnish with a pair of cherries looped over the
rim of the glass so that one cherry sinks into the cocktail, leaving
the other hanging on the outside. An alternative garnish could be
a folded orange slice and a cherry impaled on a cocktail stick and
placed across the top of the glass.

14½ oz/411g tin peaches
(slices or halves) in natural
juice
About 1 tablespoon dark rum
1½-2 tablespoons maple syrup
¼ pint/140ml soda water
4 pairs of fresh cherries

1 Liquidize the peaches and their juice with rum and
maple syrup to taste. Bear in mind that the drink will
be diluted when served.
2 Refrigerate for at least one hour or chill in the
freezer for a maximum of 20 minutes.
3 Just before serving stir in the soda water. Pour into
wine glasses and garnish with the cherries. Place the
glasses on saucers lined with a tiny paper doily.

Peach Glory

Add a few redcurrants when they are in season and increase the
honey for added sweetness.

4 large fresh peaches
¼ pint/140ml low-fat natural
yogurt
1 tablespoon clear honey
Pinch grated nutmeg
8 oz/225g blackberries
1 tablespoon chopped pistachio
nuts

1 Rinse, dry, halve and stone the peaches, but do
not peel. Place one peach half, hollow side up, on
each of four individual plates.

2 Cut up the remaining peaches and purée them in
the blender with the yogurt, honey and nutmeg.

3 Pile the blackberries on to the peach halves and
sprinkle with pistachios. Spoon the purée around the
peaches.

Pineapple and Kirsch Flambé

Choose small ripe fruit, but check that there are no soft dark
brown patches. Unfortunately few pineapples have a good flavour
— sniff the fruit before you buy and try to pick one which has at
least some bouquet. To flambé successfully, the fruit must be hot
and the Kirsch sufficiently warm. Be sure not to overheat if using
the microwave method.

1 small pineapple
2-3 tablespoons icing sugar
About 1 oz/30g unsalted
butter
4 tablespoons Kirsch

1 Cut away the top and bottom of the pineapple.
Stand the pineapple on a non-slip board and peel
with a stainless steel kitchen knife. Work from the top
of the fruit, following the curve. Remove obstinate
bits with a sharp knife.

2 Slice the pineapple and remove the tough centre
with an apple corer. Dust the slices with the icing
sugar.

3 When ready to serve, melt the butter until foaming
in a heavy frying-pan. Add the pineapple and sauté
for 1 minute, turn the slices over and cook for a
further minute.

4 Transfer to a heated serving dish, cover and take to
the table. Heat the Kirsch in a small saucepan or in a
cup in the microwave for about 30 seconds. Quickly
carry to the table.

5 Remove the cover from the pineapple, pour the
Kirsch over and ignite immediately.

Pink Yogurt

Use attractive glass goblets for best effect. Ring the changes by
using strawberries, blackberries or freshly stewed apricots.

*½ pint/280ml thick set
natural yogurt
¼ pint/140ml double cream
1 teaspoon gin
About 1 tablespoon golden
syrup
8 oz/225g raspberries
Pompadour ice-cream wafers*

1 Purée or liquidize the yogurt, cream, gin, golden
syrup and half the raspberries. Taste and add more
syrup if you wish.
2 Pour a little of the purée into four goblets, then top
with a few whole raspberries. Repeat the layering and
finish with raspberries.
3 Chill for at least ½ hour. Serve with fan-shaped
ice-cream wafers.

Rumtopf

Like the magic pot this need never empty. A rumtopf is a large
earthenware container with a lid. It needs the lid to keep out the
dust and keep in the alcohol over the six years it is claimed that the
dessert fruits will keep. You can keep it that long but you musn't be
tempted to serve the fruits in less than a month, which is the time
it takes for adequate absorption. Any glazed earthenware or glass
casserole can be used but it must be large enough. As time goes by,
the ratio of liquor to fruit will increase. Use this by storing in a
bottle and serving as a cocktail or for making jams. Select any of
the fruit from the ingredients, fresh or frozen.

*Strawberries
Raspberries
Redcurrants
Loganberries
Blackberries
Peaches
Apricots
Nectarines
Mangoes
Paw-paw
Pineapple*

*Raw cane granulated sugar
Rum
Brandy*

Optional Advance Preparations

About 1 year ahead

1 Start to assemble the rumtopf as the fruit comes
into season. Do not worry about variegated colours as
during soaking all the fruit turns somewhat red. Buy
about 1 lb/455g of a selection of six fruits.
2 Peel where absolutely necessary such as mango,
paw-paw and pineapple, but otherwise put in the fruit
unpeeled. Remove all the stones from the fruit. Trim,
top and tail red- and blackcurrants and gooseberries.
Cut up or slice all fruit that is larger than berry size.
3 Layer the fruits about 1 inch/2.5cm deep, soaking
each with two or three tablespoons rum and 1

tablespoon brandy. Cover with an equally thick layer of sugar. Repeat the layers, making sure that the fruit is always completely covered.

4 Cover tightly with a lid. Top up with more fruit as it becomes available, repeating the sugar and rum and brandy treatment.

5 When the pot is full, add the occasional tot of rum and brandy, but *not* more sugar or the fruit will become unbearably sweet. Keep in a cool place if possible.

2-3 hours before each dinner party

6 Put the pot in the refrigerator.

To assemble

7 Serve small portions only as the dessert is very potent. Bring the pot to the table for effect and dish with a soup ladle into small bowls.

Sliced Fresh Mango and Lime

NC   Serves 4-5
Takes about 15 minutes

There is no easy way to peel a mango. If the fruit is sufficiently firm halve it lengthwise around the stone, then gently swivel the two halves. They should separate easily, leaving the stone in one half. Loosen the stone with a sharp knife and remove it. Place the mango halves skin-side down, carve the flesh off the skin with a sharp knife held with the blade horizontal and cut away from the hand in slices, holding the mango steady.

1 fresh lime
3 ripe mangoes

1 Wipe the lime and grate the zest. Squeeze the juice.

2 Peel and slice the mangoes and arrange in overlapping slices on individual plates. Sprinkle with lime juice and decorate with the grated zest.

3 Chill for 15 minutes before serving.

Spotted Dick, Oven Baked _____PA Serves 5-6

Unfortunately vegetarians cannot eat this traditional British dessert
when dining out because the major ingredient is suet. Cook it at
home with vegetarian suet and wholemeal flour and you will please
everybody. If you are preparing this recipe fresh, omit the 30
minutes' reheating time. The pudding is baked to save the busy
cook from pot watching.

*2 oz/55g wholemeal
breadcrumbs
6 oz/170g wholemeal self-
raising flour
1 tablespoon baking powder
1 oz/30g light soft brown sugar
3 oz/85g mixed raisins,
sultanas and currants
5 oz/140g shredded vegetable
suet
About ¼ pint/140ml water
4 tablespoons sieved apricot
jam
4 tablespoons water*

Optional Advance Preparations

Up to 3 months ahead

1 Mix the breadcrumbs, flour and baking powder
thoroughly together, then stir in the sugar, fruit and
suet. Add sufficient cold water to mix a very soft
dough.
2 With floured hands form into a sausage shape
about the size of a small French loaf. Wrap up loosely
in well greased foil and place on a baking tray.
3 Bake in a moderate oven 350°F/180°C/Gas Mark
4 for 45 minutes. Leave to cool down, then overwrap
in another piece of foil and freeze.

To assemble

4 About 1 hour ahead remove the outer foil and
transfer the pudding (still wrapped in the foil) to a
baking tray. Bake in a moderate oven 375°F/190°C/
Gas Mark 5 for 30 minutes to thaw and reheat, open
out the foil and bake for a further 10 minutes.
5 Meanwhile warm the jam and water until blended
and pour over the hot pudding. Serve at once.

Tuilles with Chocolate Mousse _____PA Serves 8

Tuilles are very effective when shaped as little baskets. The mousse
is easy to prepare. Both keep well stored separately.

Mousse

*6 oz/170g plain dessert
chocolate
3 large eggs
1 tablespoon Cointreau
Violet petals*

Tuilles

*2 egg whites
4 oz/115g caster sugar
2 oz/55g plain flour
½ teaspoon vanilla essence
2 oz/55g flaked almonds
2 oz/55g soft margarine*

Optional Advance Preparations

Up to 2 months ahead

1 Break up the chocolate and melt in a bowl over
hot water or in the microwave. Remove from the
heat.

2 Separate the eggs, whisk the egg whites until stiff;
beat the egg yolks and *Cointreau* and strain into the
slightly cooled melted chocolate.

3 Fold in the beaten whites until no white specks
remain. Turn into a suitable container, cover and
freeze.

Up to 1 month ahead

4 Line two large baking trays with non-stick baking
parchment.

5 Whisk the egg whites until stiff. Beat in the sugar
until stiff again. Fold in the flour, then add the vanilla
essence and almonds.

6 Melt the margarine, dribble over the mixture and
fold in thoroughly. Drop the mixture in tablespoons
on to prepared trays and spread them to thin rounds,
making sure that they are well spaced out.

7 Bake in a moderately hot oven 375°F/190°C/Gas
Mark 5 for 5-10 minutes until golden. Leave for 20
seconds, then remove with a palette knife and place
over an upturned tumbler or mug. Curve over with
the hands to form a basket. Bake the remaining tuilles
in the same way, then store all in an airtight tin.

To assemble

8 Scoop the mousse into the open tuilles and
decorate with violet petals.

7 Menus

Putting together a menu is rather like a jigsaw puzzle. If the pieces do not fit it is frustrating and time-consuming and in the end you give up trying.

In the main chapters the recipes are divided into three categories — no cook, quick cook and prepare ahead dishes. These must be mixed and matched so that they fit the three golden rules of menu planning.

1 Unless it is the height of summer do not serve an entirely cold meal.
2 Never attempt to serve three consecutive hot courses. Hot and cold dishes, however, need not alternate.
3 Make sure that the courses vary in both texture and colour. Do not repeat main ingredients in other courses and try not to repeat food types, for example fruit in all three courses would not be acceptable.

As menu planning is difficult at the best of times it is particularly so for the vegetarian who must limit his choice to fruit, vegetables, pulses, grains, nuts and dairy produce. Thus some repetition is bound to occur. Non-vegetarians have a wider choice since they also eat meat, poultry, fish and seafood.

The menus in this chapter have been put together to suit the vegetarian but can also form the basis of a dinner for all discerning people. Meat-eaters need only add non-vegetarian dishes of their choice.

Guests may not always arrive at the expected time and should there be a delay a hot starter, unless it is a quick cook, a reheated one or soup, may deteriorate.

You can prepare a cold starter beforehand and even have it ready and garnished on the place mats at the table to await your guests. Cold main courses must nearly always consist of salads. Choose hot main courses from the quick cook or prepare ahead sections. I developed desserts that could be either prepared or finished off in between the courses. They can also stay in a warm oven without mishap. Cold desserts are of course reasonably trouble-free.

When entertaining several guests prepare an additional main course and the variety will be greater and you can serve smaller portions from each. To augment the meal serve additional plain vegetables or simple green salads, crusty bread, a cheese board, fresh fruit and petits fours or chocolate mints.

Consider the order of work a suggestion only. Preparation must obviously be slotted in at moments to suit yourself. You need not follow the menu selections rigidly. There are some excellent gourmet tins of soup about and when pressed for time there is no reason why you should not use ready-prepared salads and 'bought in' gateaux or ice-cream which, incidentally, can be served slightly warmed as a sauce.

The thirty menu suggestions include all the starters and desserts but by no means all the main courses. Use those not included to build your own menus.

Menu No. 1

Gaspacho
(page 54)

Yorkshire Coracles
(page 137)

Crunchy Fruit Salad
(page 144)

Drinks: *Silvaner is a fruity
and sharp white wine from the
Alsace.*

Up to 6 hours ahead: Prepare Crunchy Fruit Salad,
omitting the crumbs.

Up to 3 hours ahead: If Gaspacho is frozen, remove
from the freezer and defrost in the refrigerator. Keep
cold.

Up to 3 hours ahead: Prepare the batter for the
Yorkshire Coracles. Remove the frozen croûtons from
the freezer and place on a baking tray or prepare fresh
croûtons.

30 minutes ahead: Prepare the filling for the
Yorkshire Coracles. Remove from the heat. Toast the
millet flakes.

10 minutes before serving the starter: Decorate
the fruit salad. Heat the oil for the batter. Reheat the
croûtons.

While eating the starter: Bake the Yorkshire
Coracles and reheat the filling on minimum heat.

Menu No. 2

Mushroom and Beansprout
Soup (page 59)

Pear and Cheddar Salad
(page 113)

Marmalade Roll
(pages 148-9)

Drinks: *Burgundy is where the
really big full bodied wines are
made. Try the Côte de Nuits
area where Nuit Saint Georges
comes from, one of the most
famous red wines.*

2 hours ahead: Remove the Marmalade Roll from
the freezer and defrost in the refrigerator.

¾ hour ahead: Bake the Marmalade Roll. Prepare
the Mushroom and Beansprout Soup. While the
soup is simmering prepare the salad.

Just before serving: Garnish the salad with pear
wedges.

Menu No. 3 _____

Camembert Soufflé Glacé
(page 50)

Hot Mushroom and Batavia
Salad (page 99)

Sliced Fresh Mango and Lime
(page 153)

Drinks: A more delicate red
wine such as Beaujolais will
enhance the flavour of the
main course.

Up to 24 hours ahead: Prepare the dressing (it will need shaking well before using).

Up to 24 hours ahead: Prepare the Camembert Soufflé and store in the refrigerator.

Up to 12 hours ahead: Prepare the dessert, using a stainless steel knife. Chill in the top of the freezer.

Up to 4 hours ahead: Wash and drain the lettuce, spin well and keep in a covered container in the bottom of the refrigerator. The cheese can be grated and kept in the freezer until required or use previously frozen grated cheese by transferring to the refrigerator to defrost.

1 hour ahead: Sauté the mushrooms and garlic, switch off the heat and cover the pan and leave until ready for use.

Menu No. 4 _____

Tomato Salad
(page 62)

Green Meadow Basket
(page 92)

Caribbean Bananas
(page 142)

Drinks: Serve Muscadet, a
crisp white wine which comes
from the Loire Valley.

Up to 48 hours ahead: Prepare the potato shreds for the Green Meadow Basket and store.

Up to 24 hours ahead: Prepare the sauce for the filling. Refrigerate.

Up to 12 hours ahead: Prepare the Tomato Salad. Sprinkle with oil just prior to serving.

30 minutes ahead: Cook the broccoli for the filling, reheat the sauce and assemble the filling. Arrange the potato in nests on an ovenproof dish. Prepare the syrup for the bananas but do not peel the bananas.

While clearing away the starter: Finish the main course.

While clearing away the main course: Finish the dessert or the dish can be prepared at the table if a fondue 'base' is available.

Menu No. 5 _____

Baked Potato Skins with Dill Dunkers (page 48)

Several hours ahead: Prepare the ingredients for the salad but do not mix. Liquidize the tomatoes, mayonnaise and prunes and place in the refrigerator.

Red Salad (page 118)

Up to 2 hours ahead: Cook the syrup for the bananas. Boil for 1 minute only and leave in the saucepan. Squeeze the lemon juice on to the plate but keep covered.

Bananes au Citron (page 141)

15 minutes before serving: Bake the pre-cooked potato skins and assemble the sauce, then complete and assemble the Red Salad.

Drinks: A ginger-beer shandy preferably made with freshly drawn beer from the pub next door will go well with this menu.

After serving the main course: Reheat the syrup and cook to boil for 1 minute. Peel the bananas and complete the recipe.

Menu No. 6 _____

Fried Banana Crisps (page 53)

2 weeks ahead: Make and cook the pastry and freeze.

2 hours ahead: Assemble the flan.

Courgette, Celery and Borlotti Salad (page 82)

Up to 2 hours ahead: Prepare the vegetables for the salad but do not cook. Place in a pan with water and garlic ready for cooking.

Apple and Fig Flan (page 140)

Not more than 1 hour ahead: Cook the Banana Crisps.

Just before serving the dinner: Complete the salad.

Drinks: Rosé is a wine often frowned upon by the connoisseurs and this is nonsense, particularly if the non-sparkling type is chosen such as a Tavel from the Rhône Valley.

Menu No. 7 _____

Grapefruit, Date and Cashew Nut Indienne (page 54)

Swiss Asparagus Roulade (page 130)

Peach Glory (page 151)

Drinks: *As the main course is somewhat bland a light white wine such as a Piesporter will go well.*

Up to 24 hours ahead: Prepare the cheese sauce for the roulade. Cover, cool and store. Prepare the breadcrumb and egg yolk sauce. Cover and refrigerate.

Up to 12 hours ahead: Prepare the grapefruit and dates. Arrange on individual plates, cover and refrigerate. Do not stack the plates one on top of the other. Chop and mix the nuts with the cheese. Cover and refrigerate.

1 hour ahead: Complete the starter by decorating with the cheese, dust with the cardamom and refrigerate until required.

45 minutes ahead: Prepare and cook the roulade. Ensure a hot serving dish is available. Prepare the dessert, reserving the garnish.

10 minutes ahead: Assemble the roulade and keep hot.

Immediately before serving the dessert: Garnish.

Menu No. 8 _____

Celery and Blue Cheese Soup (page 52)

Salade Toutes Saisons (page 125)

Edwardian Blackcurrant Pudding (page 144)

Drinks: *Pimms No. 1 is a very refreshing drink and particularly welcome on a warm summer's evening.*

2 hours ahead: Prepare the salad items but do not assemble. Cook the potato and grate any ingredients if to be used in the salad.

1 hour ahead: Thaw the soup. Gather the ingredients for the dessert. Put the fruit, honey and spice in the dish. Separately mix the sugar, suet and breadcrumbs together.

Just before the meal: Place the crumbs on the fruit and set to bake.

Immediately before serving the starter: Complete the soup.

Just before serving the main course: Assemble and complete the salad.

Menu No. 9 _____

*Water Melon and Raspberry
Soup (page 63)*

*Dolmades
(page 86–7)*

*Tuilles with Chocolate Mousse
(page 155)*

*Drinks: Retsina has a bitter
taste if it is at all old so drink
whilst really young, the best
Retsina coming from the
Attica area.*

1–2 hours ahead: Remove the mousse from the
freezer and place in the refrigerator.
30 minutes ahead: Reheat the Dolmades.
15 minutes ahead: Prepare the sauce and the olive
and Feta cheese salad.
Just before the meal: Fill the tuilles and decorate.

Menu No. 10 _____

*Guacamole-stuffed Tomatoes
(page 163)*

*Vegetable Gratin
(page 132)*

*Pineapple and Kirsch Flambé
(page 151)*

*Drinks: Rioja is a really full-
bodied red which is Spain's
most popular wine in this
country.*

Up to 12 hours ahead: Prepare and refrigerate all
the ingredients for the Guacamole-stuffed Tomatoes
except the avocado and keep the lime slices on a
covered plate to prevent drying out. Prepare and slice
the pineapple. Cover and refrigerate.
1 hour ahead: Complete the stuffed tomato recipe.
Place in the refrigerator.
¾ hour in advance: Assemble the Vegetable
Gratin.
About 15 minutes before the meal: Dust the
pineapple with the icing sugar and put the butter in
the pan.
Just before serving the starter: Put the Vegetable
Gratin in the oven set at 350°F/180°C/Gas Mark 4.
Sprinkle with the almonds after baking.
After the main course: Sauté the pineapple and
flambé at the table if you have a fondue flamer.

Menu No. 11

Lemon Mint and Lime Water Ice (page 58)

Enchiladas Sante Fé (page 88)

Caribbean Bananas (page 142)

Drinks: What about a glass or two of tequila?

Up to 24 hours ahead: Make the tomato and herbs for the main course filling and refrigerate. Make certain the tortillas/pitta bread are ready.

1 hour ahead: Complete the topping and bake just before bringing the starter to the table. Prepare the syrup for the bananas and complete the recipe after the main course has been cleared away.

15 minutes before serving: Remove the water ice from the freezer.

Menu No. 12

Tomato Salad (page 62)

Wild Rice Salad (page 136)

Crêpes Suzette (page 142-3)

Drinks: Chinese tea is most refreshing and even if you don't go through the full ritual you should try to learn some of the tricks of the elegant tea-drinking customs.

Up to 24 hours ahead: Make the dressing for the salad. Cook the rice and vegetables and store in the refrigerator. Prepare the Brazil nuts.

Up to 12 hours ahead: Prepare the tomato salad but reserve the oil.

Up to 1 hour ahead: Wash and prepare the lettuce, bring the rice and vegetables to room temperature and complete the dish.

After serving the main course: Complete and assemble the crêpes.

Menu No. 13

Fresh Pears with Walnut Sauce
(page 53)

Aubergine Soufflé
(page 69)

Jubilee Cherries
(page 147)

Drinks: Aubergine has a very distinctive flavour and tends to destroy too light a wine. A glass of sherry and then lemonade with the meal will be suitable.

Up to 24 hours ahead: Mix the mayonnaise, yogurt and honey for the starter. Prepare the garnish, cover with cling film and refrigerate. Chill the avocado dishes.

1¼ hours ahead: Partly prepare the Jubilee Cherries, drain, make up the juice and mix in the arrowroot but do not cook at this stage.

1 hour ahead: Assemble the Aubergine Soufflé and bake. As soon as the soufflé is in the oven, prepare and serve the starter so that the soufflé can be brought to the table and eaten immediately.

After the main course has been served: Complete the dessert.

Menu No. 14

Orange Flowers
(page 60)

Hazelnut Steaks in Sorrel Sauce (page 96)

Apricot and Raisin Mousse
(page 141)

Drinks: Red wine accompanies nuts to perfection and the Hungarian Egri Bikaver might be great fun.

24 hours ahead: Prepare the mousse, as the colour darkens and the flavour improves during that time. Decorate up to half an hour before the meal.

Up to 12 hours ahead: Prepare the oranges, keep covered in the refrigerator and garnish just before serving.

15 minutes ahead: Cook the steaks and keep warm. Heat the sauce and keep this warm too.

Just before serving: Garnish.

Menu No. 15

Grapefruit, Date and Cashew Nut Indienne (page 54)

Asparagus and Cucumber Omelette (page 68)

Pineapple and Kirsch Flambé (page 151)

Drinks: *The light bouquet and spicy flavour of a Gewürtztraminer from the Alsace would be ideal.*

Up to 12 hours ahead: Prepare the grapefruit and dates. Arrange on individual plates, cover and refrigerate. Do not stack the plates one on top of the other. Chop the nuts and mix with the cheese. Cover and refrigerate. Prepare and slice the pineapple and cover that and refrigerate.

1 hour ahead: Complete the starter by decorating with the cheese, dust with the cardamom and store in the refrigerator.

45 minutes ahead: Dust the pineapple with icing sugar. Cook fresh asparagus, prepare the tinned asparagus sauce and separate the eggs.

After clearing away the starter: Complete the omelette. Finish the pineapple by sautéing or use a fondue flamer at the table.

Menu No. 16

Leek and Lovage Salad (page 57)

Devilish Mushrooms (page 86)

Sliced Fresh Mango and Lime (page 153)

Drinks: *Be a real devil and try a little pink champagne. If you can't afford the real stuff try a wine from Saumur.*

Up to 24 hours ahead: Prepare the bread cases for the mushrooms. Prepare the sliced fresh mango and lime, arrange on plates, cover and chill. Do not stack the plates.

30 minutes ahead: Complete the Leek and Lovage Salad.

Just before serving the starter: Cook the mushrooms and fill the bread cases. Prepare a moderate oven but do not bake. Prepare the sauce but do not heat.

While eating the starter: Bake the mushroom bread cases and heat the sauce just before serving.

Menu No. 17

Beetroot in Orange Vinaigrette
(page 49)

Pancakes Blé Noir
(page 111)

Peach Glory
(page 151)

Drinks: Brittany is one of the few districts in France that doesn't make wine, so why not accompany this dinner with sparkling fresh cider, from just across the Channel?

Up to 48 hours ahead: Make the pancakes and keep covered in the refrigerator. Make the filling and refrigerate.
Up to 24 hours ahead: Prepare the vinaigrette for the beetroot.
1 hour ahead: Complete the beetroot, place on alfalfa and pour over the vinaigrette just before serving. Prepare the peaches and purée for the dessert and keep refrigerated.
15 minutes ahead: Spread the pancakes with the cheese filling. Fold, arrange in the dish and cover with the topping.
After the starter is eaten: Grill the pancakes. Complete the Peach Glory.

Menu No. 18

Celery and Carrot Cream Slaw (page 51)

Imam Bayeldi (page 100-101)

Pink Yogurt (page 152)

Drinks: Muslims do not normally drink alcohol and a sherbert would be a grand accompaniment to this meal.

Up to 24 hours ahead: Prepare the pink yogurt. Reserve the raspberries for final decoration. Chill but do not freeze. At the same time mix the ingredients for the slaw and prepare the Imam Bayeldi according to the recipe.
1 hour ahead: Complete the bayeldi with minimum heat under the pan. Prepare the rice or pitta if being served. Arrange the slaw on the lettuce and garnish with parsley. Place the final garnish on the yogurt.

Menu No. 19

Melon, Ginger and Kiwi Petals (page 59)

Baked Avocado (page 70)

Grand Marnier Mousse en *(Boîte (page 146-7)*

Drinks: *As a liqueur is already cited in the recipe I can think of nothing more refreshing than iced tea.*

24 hours ahead: Refrigerate the melon and slice the ginger. Put the kiwi fruit in the bottom of the refrigerator.

1 hour ahead: Unmould the mousse into the meringue case and keep refrigerated. Prepare orange segment garnish for the mousse but do not decorate yet. Complete the melon, ginger and kiwi petals and place in the refrigerator. Prepare the avocado and bulgur cracked wheat if being used.

Just before serving the starter: Bake.

Before serving the dessert: Decorate the mousse with orange segments.

Menu No. 20

Pineapple and Walnut Pâté (page 60)

Ginger Tofu Chow Mein (page 91)

Malakoff Torte (page 148)

Drinks: *The ginger will take away the value of most wines so serve a plain glass of beer with the chow mein and then a heady glass of port with the torte.*

24 hours ahead: Prepare the pâté but do not garnish. Make the Melba toast.

Up to 12 hours ahead: Mix the vegetables and mayonnaise for the ginger tofu.

1 hour ahead: Turn out the torte and leave in a cool place. Decorate the top with glacé cherries when soft.

30 minutes ahead: Cook the noodles and tofu and keep warm in a low oven if necessary. Garnish the pâté with fresh dill weed.

Just before serving the main course: Assemble the chow mein.

Menu No. 21

Asparagus with Yogurt and Chive Dressing (page 47)

Falafel (page 89)

Jubilee Cherries (page 147)

Drinks: *Chianti bottles are more difficult to find now with their traditional wicker coverings but the wine remains the same.*

Up to 24 hours ahead: Cook the soaked chick peas. Prepare the bulgur cracked wheat and follow the recipe instructions to prepare the chick-pea paste.
1¼ hours ahead: Prepare the Jubilee Cherries, drain, make up the juice and mix in the arrowroot but do not cook at this stage. Shape the chick-pea paste and refrigerate.
30 minutes ahead: While the asparagus is cooking fry the Falafel. Drain and keep warm. Complete the starter.
After the main course has been served: Complete the dessert.

Menu No. 22

American Grapefruit (page 46-7)

Provençale Crumble (page 116)

Iced Coffee Mousse (page 147)

Drinks: *One of the heaviest red wines you can choose is a Châteauneuf-du-Pape which will augment this main course well.*

Up to 2 months ahead: Prepare and freeze separately the vegetable casserole and the topping.
24 hours ahead: Prepare the Iced Coffee Mousse and freeze.
2 hours ahead: Remove the vegetable casserole and crumb topping from the freezer. Sprinkle the topping over the vegetables.
30 minutes ahead: Bake the main course and prepare the starter.
15 minutes ahead: Defrost the dessert at room temperature.

Menu No. 23_____

Pumpkin Soup
(pages 60–61)

Kashiri Salad
(page 102)

Caribbean Bananas
(page 142)

Drinks: *The flavour of curry does not match well with wine and a can of lager is the best accompaniment.*

Up to 1 month ahead: Prepare and freeze the soup.
24 hours ahead: Prepare the dressing for the salad, omitting the coriander leaves at this stage. Allow the soup to defrost in the refrigerator.
30 minutes ahead: Complete the salad and the accompaniments.
15 minutes ahead: Heat the soup, add the yogurt and garnish. Prepare the syrup for the dessert. Do not peel the bananas.
After clearing away the main course: Finish the dessert. This can be done at the table if a fondue flamer is available.

Menu No. 24_____

Iced Cucumber Soup
(page 56)

American Corn Fritters with Broccoli Purée (page 67)

Orange Brulette
(page 150)

Drinks: *Refreshing cola straight from the refrigerator.*

Up to 24 hours ahead: Prepare the broccoli purée. Cool and refrigerate. Chop the dates and prepare the orange for the dessert. Blend the yogurt and honey. Store in the refrigerator.
1¼ hours ahead: Prepare the starter and refrigerate.
1 hour ahead: Prepare the pear, mix with the orange, dates and yogurt and honey mixture. Divide into ramekins and chill. Prepare the dessert topping. Prepare and cook the fritters. Keep warm in a serving dish in a moderate oven.
Just before serving the starter: Garnish.
While clearing away the starter: Reheat the broccoli purée.
After clearing away the main course: Complete the dessert.

Menu No. 25

Hummus
(page 56)

Brussels Sprouts Amandine
with Hot Tabbouleh
(page 73)

Fresh Fruit Salad
(page 145)

Drinks: *Serve with iced lime
juice, preferably with a few
slices of fresh lime floating in
each tumbler.*

Up to 48 hours ahead: Prepare and refrigerate the
bulgur cracked wheat for the Tabbouleh.
Up to 24 hours ahead: Prepare and refrigerate the
Amandine.
2 hours ahead: Prepare the Hummus and spread on
serving plates. Keep in a cool place.
1 hour ahead: Prepare the fruit salad and refrigerate.
20 minutes ahead: Assemble the main course and
keep hot.
Just before serving the starter: Garnish.
Just before serving the main course: Garnish.

Menu No. 26

Spring Cocktail
(page 62)

Chequerboard Grill with Port
and Carrot Purée (page 77)

Rumtopf
(page 152)

Drinks: *There is a
considerable amount of liquor
in this menu but a light red
wine such as a young
Beaujolais will contrast well.*

Up to 24 hours ahead: Prepare the nut patties,
carefully following the recipe instructions. Prepare the
purée. Refrigerate the patties and the purée.
3 hours ahead: Refrigerate the Rumtopf.
45 minutes ahead: Prepare the Spring Cocktail.
Chill for 30 minutes.
15 minutes ahead: Assemble and bake the main
course.
While eating the starter course: Reheat the purée.
After clearing the main course: Serve the
Rumtopf straight from the pot at the table into
individual dishes.

Menu No. 27

Grilled Grapefruit in Port
(page 55)

Palm Hearts St Jacques
(pages 110–111)

Spotted Dick, Oven Baked
(page 154)

Drinks: *Whatever may be*
served for the first two courses,
a glass of port, preferably
vintage, will go well with the
dessert.

Up to 24 hours ahead: Prepare the potato and pipe around shells or dishes. Prepare the palm hearts and cook the sauce. Refrigerate.
1 hour ahead: Prepare and bake the Spotted Dick or follow the recipe instructions if reheating from frozen.
15 minutes ahead: Heat the grill. Prepare the grapefruit. Heat the palm hearts and the sauce for the main course. Grill the grapefruit. Arrange the palm hearts in prepared dishes. Fetch the sauce and pour over.
While clearing the starter: Grill the main course.
While clearing the main course: Gently heat the jam with the water for the dessert.

Menu No. 28

Sesame Seed Fingers with
Tahini Dip (page 61)

Moroccan Salad
(page 105)

Peach Daiquiri
(page 150)

Drinks: *A fresh fruit cup well*
chilled and freshened just
before serving with lemonade
or soda water is all that is
needed for this menu.

24 hours ahead: Cook the soaked chestnuts and rice. Drain and chop the chestnuts and mix with the oils, vinegar, coriander, pepper and sultanas. Refrigerate.
12 hours ahead: Prepare the tomatoes, fill and refrigerate.
1 hour ahead: Prepare the dessert to refrigeration stage.
30 minutes ahead: Prepare and cook the starter.
Just before serving the main course: Place the tomatoes on a base of freshly shredded lettuce.
After clearing the main course: Finish the dessert and garnish.

Menu No. 29

Artichauds au Citron Vert
(pages 46-7)

Hot Boursin Rolls
(page 98)

Crunchy Fruit Salad
(page 144)

Drinks: Liebfraumilch is a
slightly sweet white German
wine which matches cheese
dishes admirably.

Up to 24 hours ahead: Prepare the rolls, wrap and refrigerate.

Up to 6 hours ahead: Prepare the dessert but do not sprinkle with the crumbs.

1 hour ahead: Prepare and cook the starter.

30 minutes ahead: Prepare the mushrooms and put ready in the oven with foil-wrapped rolls but do not heat the oven yet. Complete the dessert and decorate. Complete the starter. Heat the oven and bake the Boursin-filled rolls for 5 minutes.

Just before serving the starter: Open up the top of the foil packets, sprinkle the rolls with sesame seeds and switch off the oven.

Menu No. 30

Leek and Lovage Salad
(page 57)

Parsleyed Potatoes with
Courgette and Red Wine
Casserole (page 112)

Tuiles with Chocolate Mousse
(page 155)

Drinks: As a final fling a well
chilled bottle of champagne
will make this a sparkling
meal.

Up to 48 hours ahead: Prepare and cook the tuiles. Store in an airtight tin. Prepare the chocolate mousse and freeze.

Up to 12 hours ahead: Prepare the leeks and radish garnish for the starter. Cover and refrigerate.

2 hours ahead: Season the yogurt and mix with marinated leeks. Keep cool.

45 minutes ahead: Cook the main course. While the dish is cooking assemble the starter and garnish.

After clearing the main course: Assemble and garnish the dessert.

Index